DIGITAL MATERIALITY
IN ARCHITECTURE
GRAMAZIO & KOHLER

DIGITAL MATERIALITY IN ARCHITECTURE
GRAMAZIO & KOHLER
LARS MÜLLER PUBLISHERS

7   Digital Materiality in Architecture
    Fabio Gramazio and Matthias Kohler

12 HOW MUCH FREEDOM CAN YOU HANDLE?
    mTable, Table Series, 2002

16 WAVE OVER
    Public Bath, Locarno, Competition 2006

18 1 CM OF INFORMATION, 7 TONS OF CONCRETE
    Interference Cube, Swiss Art Awards, Art Basel, 2003

22 SUPERWOOD
    Wood Carvings, Restaurant of the Monte Rosa Alpine Hut, 2008–2009

24 UNDER MY SKIN
    sWISH*, Exhibition Pavilion at Expo.02, Biel, 2000–2002

30 VEILING
    Private House, Riedikon, 2004–2009

32 Interjections I

34 ON/OFF
    Tanzhaus, Contemporary Dance House, Zurich, 2005–2007

40 LIGHTLINE
    Polychrome Light Installation, Uster, 2006–2008

42 THE WORLD'S LARGEST TIMEPIECE
    Bahnhofstrasse Christmas Lights, Zurich, 2003–2005

49 A Short Biography of KR150 L110
    Brenda Lynn Edgar

51 Robocrop
    A Cut through the Visual History of Robotics 1921–2028
    Jules Spinatsch

57 R-O-B
    Robotic Fabrication Unit, 2007–2008

58 Interjections II

60 ADDING ON
    Research and Teaching Projects on Additive Processes, ETH Zurich

74 Interjections III

76 TAKING AWAY
    Research and Teaching Projects on Perforations, ETH Zurich

88 RUBIK
    Science City Housing, Zurich, Competition 2008

90 Interjections IV

92 HEART OF BRICKS
    Pavilion for Gallery Seroussi, Paris, Competition 2007

94 17° OF DEVIATION
    Gantenbein Vineyard Façade, Fläsch, 2006

102 STRUCTURAL OSCILLATIONS
    Installation at the 11th Venice Architecture Biennale, Swiss Pavilion, 2008

110 Credits

Among the many individuals who contributed substantially
to the work presented in this book we especially thank the following
collaborators for their commitment: Ralph Bärtschi, Tobias Bonwetsch,
Beat Ferrario, Michael Knauss, Daniel Kobel, Michael Lyrenmann,
Thomas Melliger, Silvan Oesterle.

We thank the ETH Zurich Faculty of Architecture for having provided
us the academic environment to conduct our research.

Digital Materiality in Architecture

Fabio Gramazio and Matthias Kohler

We use the term *digital materiality* to describe an emergent transformation in the expression of architecture. Materiality is increasingly being enriched with digital characteristics, which substantially affect architecture's physis. *Digital materiality* evolves through the interplay between digital and material processes in design and construction. The synthesis of two seemingly distinct worlds—the digital and the material—generates new, self-evident realities. Data and material, programming and construction are interwoven. This synthesis is enabled by the techniques of *digital fabrication,* which allows the architect to control the manufacturing process through design data. Material is thus enriched by information; material becomes "informed." In the future, architects' ideas will permeate the fabrication process in its entirety. This new situation transforms the possibilities and thus the professional scope of the architect.

Sensuality of Digital Order

Digital materiality leads to a new expression and—surprisingly enough, given the technical associations of the term "digital"—to a new sensuality in architecture. Digital and material orders enter into a dialogue, in the course of which each is enriched by the other. *Digital materiality* is thereby able to address different levels of our perception. It is characterized by an unusually large number of precisely arranged elements, a sophisticated level of detail, and the simultaneous presence of different scales of formation. Despite its intrinsic complexity, we experience and understand it intuitively. *Digital materiality* addresses our ability to recognize naturally grown organizational forms and to interpret their internal order. Its expression is novel, but not alien. *Digital materiality* is not rooted solely in the material world and its physical laws such as gravity, or in material properties. It is also enriched by the rules of the immaterial world of digital logics, such as its processual nature or calculatory precision. Digital orders intensify the particularities of materials. Materials do not appear primarily as a texture or surface, but are exposed and experienced in their whole depth and plasticity. Even familiar materials—such as bricks, which have been known for over 9000 years—appear in new ways.

For the observer, a tension spans the intuitively understandable behavior of a material and the design logic, which may not be immediately obvious. The logic can be sensed, but not necessarily explained. This obscurity seduces our senses, sending them on a voyage of discovery and inviting us to linger and reflect.

Programming Constructions

Digital materiality is generated through the integration of construction and programming in the design process. We use the conceptional affinity of the production of building components and computer programming. Today there are 700 million personal computers in use, in addition to 1.7 billion mobile phones, the latest generation of which are essentially mobile computers, plus countless other microchips built into various electronic devices. There is much that a computer cannot do; but certain things that it can do very well. It cannot substitute for the architect in the creation of designs, but is an invaluable design tool. A computer program describes the processing of data as a sequence of individual calculation steps. Similarly, the manufacturing of a building component takes place as a temporal sequence of individual steps in fabrication.

The sequence of construction steps—which step is first, which step follows—is usually not arbitrary, since they build upon one another and thus determine successive steps. This sequentiality is possibly the most radical analogy between construction, the knowledge and art of putting individual building components together as a built spatial ensemble, and computer programming. By mapping the *savoir-faire* of construction into a programmed process, we gain immediate control over digital fabrication. From now on, we are no longer designing the form that will ultimately be produced, but the production process itself. Design and execution are no longer phases in a temporal sequence—design sketches do not need to be converted into execution drawings anymore. The design incorporates the idea and knowledge of its production already at its moment of conception. In turn, the understanding of construction as an integral part of architectural design takes on greater significance. Digital craftsmanship thus continues the tradition of construction in architecture.

Does it make sense to formalize designs completely or partially in computer programs, to write down architectural logics, instead of drawing or modeling architectural forms? As architects we have had little experience of the unfamiliar "language" of programming. Many architects find it constricting, because it requires precise settings from the outset. To allow oneself to be limited by this precision would however be as pointless as capitulating before a freshly sharpened pencil. Because in reality, it is precisely programming that provides the necessary instrumental basis for liberating oneself from prevailing images of digital architecture production.

The practical, "hands-on" experience of programming demystifies digital technologies and fosters a liberated, autonomous approach to the computer. Through these practical skills we emancipate ourselves from existing CAAD tools and the passive application of their built-in paradigms and menu functions, which are mostly programmed simulations of traditional drawing processes. Instead, it is necessary to develop programming languages suitable for architecture that account for the fact that when designing, the exception is often just as important as the rule; or that hierarchical dependencies can change throughout the design process. Like spoken languages, programming languages and their paradigms are also subject to continuous change. Architects can intervene in this evolution by developing their own dialects that take up the subjects of construction, materials and space.

Building with Robots
The robot connects the digital reality of the computer with the material reality of built architecture. The simple insight that architecture is largely built through the addition of parts or the aggregation of materials allows us to advance digital fabrication. As we accumulate materials precisely at the point where they are

needed, we can weave form and function directly into building components, and are not limited to the design of their surfaces. The industrial robot enables us to implement this additive principle on an architectural scale.

Worldwide, there are currently more than a million multifunctional robots in use, predominantly articulated-arm robots, and their numbers have risen steadily since the 1980s. The industrial robot has become standard in automation precisely because, like the personal computer, it has not been optimized for one single task but is suitable for a wide spectrum of applications. Rather than being forced to operate within the predefined parameters of a specialized machine, we are able to design the actual "manual skills" of the generic robot ourselves. We do not just steer it to a particular point in space, but also determine its capacities for physical manipulation and processing. By defining the robot's hand—also called the "end-effector"—and determining its movements, we teach the robot a desired type of construction. We teach it to register its surroundings through sensors, and to affect the environment through the robot hand. The robot thus connects the world of immaterial logic with that of material construction in the most direct way.

One might ask whether and why architects should use industrial robots or even computer programming, tools that can appear architecturally irrelevant. In our opinion it is crucial that architects, now and in the future, choose their means consciously and master their tools. Accessing these generic tools enables architects to create their individual design instruments and thus generates diverse forms of expression. They will thereby be in a position to answer contemporary demands with contemporary means and concepts. The fact that no new conventions have arisen in the design and building world in recent decades shows that built architecture has so far benefited only marginally from digital technologies. Through its link to the tradition of construction, *digital materiality* changes the culture of architecture, both in its expression and in its productive capacity. Architects are predisposed to forge links between technology and the built environment.

Variation and Multiplicity
Through *digital materiality*, architecture becomes increasingly rich and diversified. This diversification affects different scales, from materials and building components to spatial sequences and loadbearing structures, to houses and urban development zoning. Variation emerges as it becomes possible to design large numbers of elements in differentiated ways using digital means. Such designs would have made very little sense before the availability of computers and digital fabrication, but their realization has now become a matter of course. The potential of digital design and production processes can best be exploited where a very large number of parts must be combined. Here they extend the architect's human capabilities; they improve his or her overview and multiply the possibilities for control of the design. In order to design a façade with hundreds of windows, for example, or a large building volume with mixed forms of housing, the architect has until now had to turn to the classical manual aids such as the grid, or to develop repeatable types. Repetition makes it possible to organize variation manually, to control and construct it with simple procedures. With the rise of *digital materiality*, the frontier between system and variation is renegotiated. As a consequence, architectures develop that place diverse, complementary logics in relation to one another.

In the digital age, our concept of serial repetition, which was the product of industrialization, is being transformed much in the same way as the opposing romantic conception of the "natural" uniqueness of craftsmanship. A language of diversity is emerging that gains its identity through the design of processes rather than final forms. In these processes, different elements combine adaptively into a coherent, harmonious whole. The multilayered, sometimes complex arrangements that constitute the aesthetics and expression of *digital materiality* may be reminiscent of the organic structures of the animal or plant world. But this comparison, though appealing, falls short: it masks the fact that digital systems do not arise out of biological conditions, and are not rooted in them either. The digital is an independent cultural achievement resulting from centuries of human engagement with logic. Precisely for this reason the computer is a fascinating instrument, one that motivates a designer to exploit the human potential for associative thinking in order to discover new organizing principles, and establish new relations with the built environment. The multiplicity that attends a design of digital processes seems novel, but not entirely strange, since it refers to familiar experiences of perception. The forms in all their variety appeal to the senses while continuing to assert their distinctly inorganic derivation.

Designing Processes
Digital materiality leads us from the design of static forms to the design of material processes. In doing so we give up geometry, whether drawn or modeled, as architecture's actual building plan and its primary basis for design decisions. Instead, we design the relationships and sequences that inhabit architecture and that emerge as its physical manifestation. But once we begin to invent such material processes, a new way of thinking about architecture reveals itself. It is a conceptual way of designing with architectural parameters, conditions, relationships, and degrees of freedom.

We ask ourselves: which parameters determine the design, and which do not, but still have an effect on its form and function? Using digital logics we define relationships and intentions in the form of rules. We weigh the influences that the design-generating factors have on each other. Through the medium of programming we can model complex decision processes, checking and refining them iteratively. Architectural expression thus takes on a different character, because new conventions emerge in the medium of programming.

In this way of conceiving architecture, processes are not mere metaphors for a process-oriented approach to design, but are concrete sequences of operations, procedures that have to be designed. These procedures are determined, they have a beginning and an end. They produce directly tangible results, the qualities of which can be tested intuitively and analytically, as we can with sketching or building models. We exploit the advantages of programming by integrating them into our traditional methods of design.

When architecture becomes the design of material processes, we no longer have a static plan in front of us, but a dynamic set of rules. We design a behavior. A set of rules like this has the advantage that even very fundamental interventions can still be implemented even late in the process, as long as they are anticipated as an open parameter in the design. We can work in a determined manner, but with open conditions that will be set only at an advanced design stage. This even offers the possibility of intentionally ceding partial control over selected design parameters to customers or partners. We thus design architecture itself as an open system with different active participants. This type of design, detached from a drive towards form, does justice both to the ever more complex conditions of our profession, and to the material substance of architecture, including its sensual qualities. Designing architecture as processes thus strengthens the central role of the architect as proactive author.

The Changed Physis of Architecture
Design using digital technologies interests us because it delineates the boundaries of rationality and of predictable reality. In our opinion, designing architecture is not an activity that can be reduced to performance optimization—it is a multifaceted cultural production. It is precisely *digital materiality* that shows us quite plainly the essentially human dimension and quality of this production. Under conditions of apparently extreme rationality, which range from computer programming to fabrication using the industrial robot, we discover associative, manifold and tangible ways to think, build and experience architecture with all our senses. We realize that the probability of encountering discoveries and innovations is increased, not limited, by using rational means of design and fabrication. Our senses are taken by surprise, as we cease designing by means of visual representations intended to be converted into buildings. Architectural expression is instead produced only in the course of the design and materialization process, and takes on its character little by little. *Digital materiality* changes the *physis* of architecture; changes the *Gestalt*, and ultimately the image that society has of architecture.

HOW MUCH FREEDOM CAN YOU HANDLE?

MTABLE, TABLE SERIES, 2002

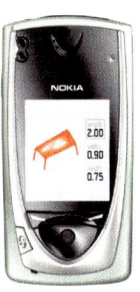

With mTable, we've created a table that customers can co-design. This light-hearted and slightly ironic project enables us to examine the consequences of customer interaction when designing non-standard products; in the process it also raises interesting questions. How much responsibility can the customer take on? Or want to take on? Who has final authorship? How far can he identify with the product? What does this open design strategy mean for architecture?

In this project we used digital communications and production technologies to custom-design and fabricate a table. We turned the mobile phone into a personal design tool, examining how it can allow individuals to co-design their physical environment. mTable shifts the focus of the act of designing, from defining a form to specifying a system. The design concept, its rules and formal consequences are carefully embedded into software that serves as the framework within which customers can develop their own creative strategies. For the first time, this gives them control over the designer's privileged domain: form.

How does it work? The principle is simple. Customers chose the table's dimensions, material and color on their mobile phone display. They can then place deformation points on the underside of the table and apply pressure on them. This turns the underside into a landscape, breaking through the top surface at points and creating holes with extremely thin edges. The program on the mobile phone regularly verifies whether the table is still structurally feasible despite the holes in it. The phone display's low resolution and the deliberately reduced functionality of the interface ensure that customers focus on the most essential design concerns. As soon as the customer is satisfied with the design, he or she can transmit the parameters defining the table as a simple series of numbers to the web platform mshape.com. Here, the table can be seen in high resolution and compared to the designs of other customers. After placing an order, the table is cut according to the mobile phone data by a computer-controlled milling machine. The virtual three-dimensional model is transcribed onto physical material.

The openings in the table top, the curved edges and spectacular underside make every table unique—admittedly only superficially, as they all share a common origin of form and concept. They are the result of individual customers' decisions and variations on the same design motif, yet together they form a single entity: the mTable design family. By deciding for themselves whether or where the holes are positioned, the customers assume partial responsibility for the aesthetic and functional efficiency of their product. However by defining the system's rules, the designer still maintains full control over which decisions are delegated to the customers and how freely they can intervene. mTable redefines the frontier between designer and customer: the customer becomes a co-designer.

WAVE OVER

PUBLIC BATH, LOCARNO, COMPETITION 2006

The public bath, which unfolds under a softly curved roof landscape, was designed exclusively using parametric force fields. Virtual, computer-generated forces influenced the underside of the raised roof slab and deformed it. This produced vaultlike spaces, glazed where they break through the ceiling and open up a view into the sky. These roof openings, framed by thin, tapering edges, fill the spaces with light. The internal walls, which enclose the main spaces, follow the course of the roof landscape and support it.

Thus, the space-defining elements—walls and roof—are derived from the position and strength of the forces acting on them. This harmonious design system generates formally similar spaces that flow into one another. However, they are strongly differentiated in their dimensions, character and level of introversion, depending on the number of generating forces and on their position in relation to the façade. This spatial differentiation allows a varied spatial program, such as the large swimming pool and the intimate wellness zones.

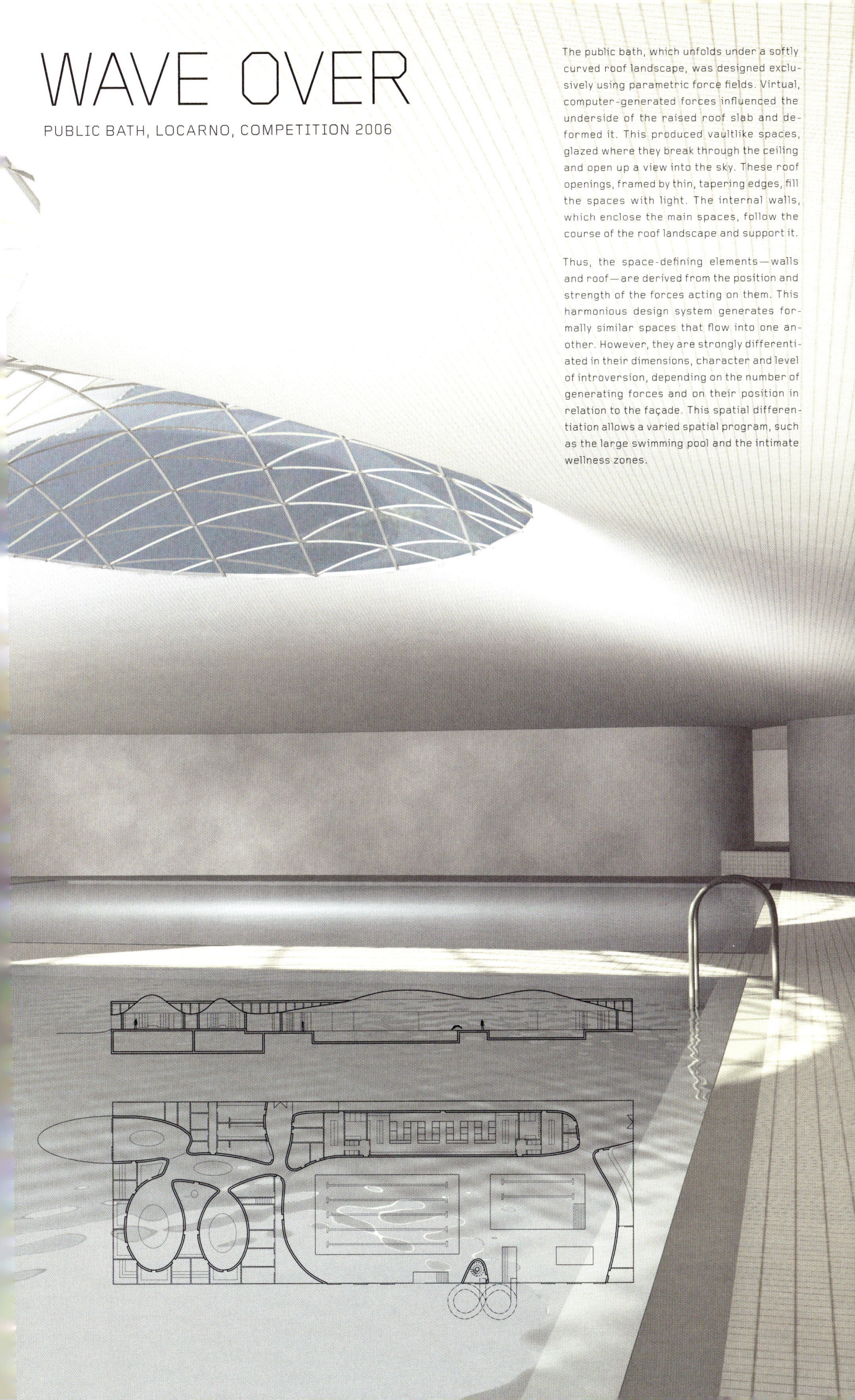

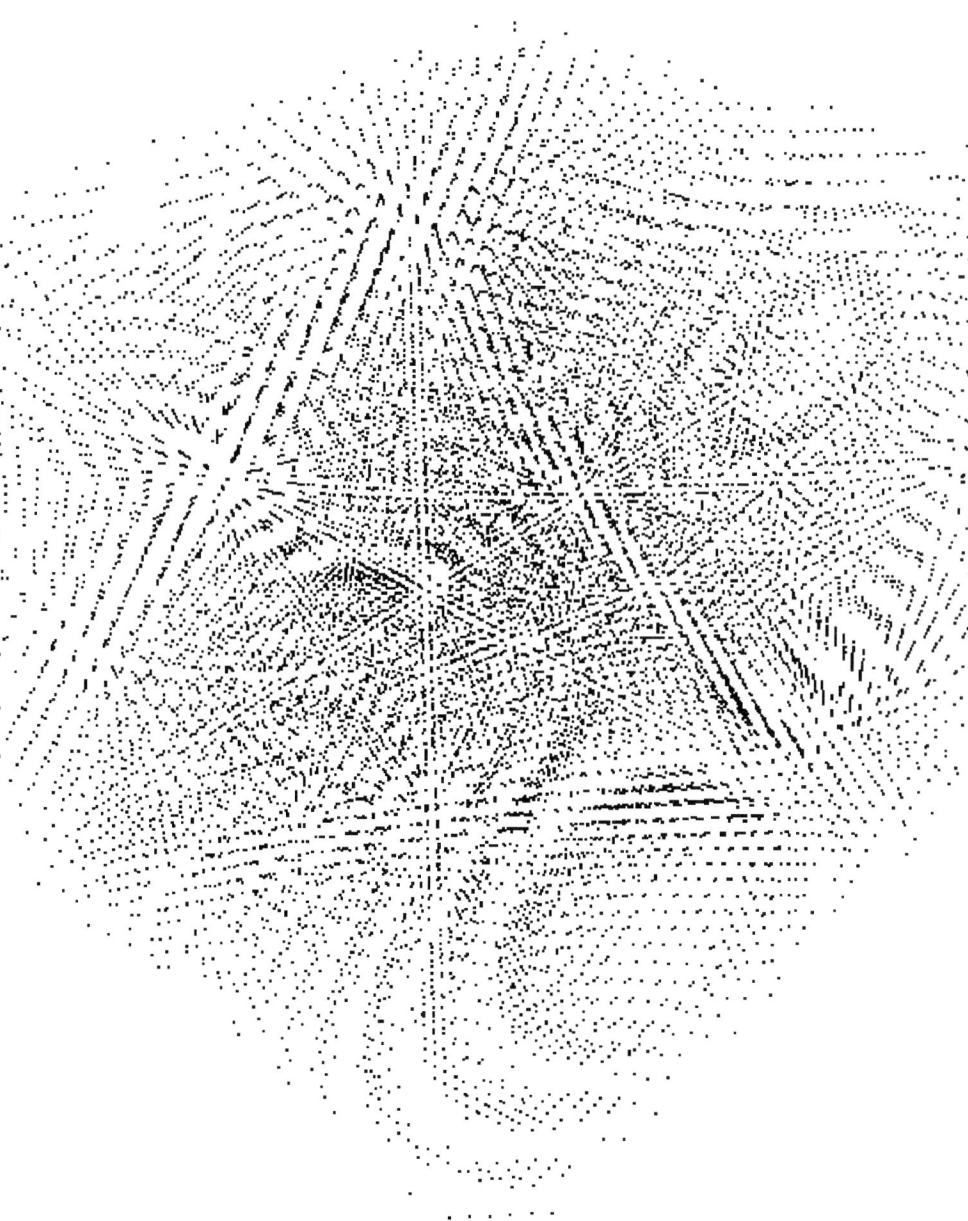

1 CM OF INFORMATION, 7 TONS OF CONCRETE

INTERFERENCE CUBE, SWISS ART AWARDS, ART BASEL, 2003

Interference Tower, Gotthard, 2004

Imagine cutting a cube out of an onion. The three-dimensional inner structure of the onion leaves a two-dimensional imprint on the surface of the cube. In the interference cube, a prototypical spatial unit that we realized for the Swiss Art Awards, we similarly outlined a virtual, spatial force field on the inner walls of a cube. In this project we explored new strategies for making patterns from spatial algorithms and superseding conventional pictorial paradigms based on two-dimensional textures.

Our spatial unit was a cube with five closed sides, each of 2.3 m. Using a computer, we placed this cube into a virtual algorithmic force field that rippled outwards in space. We then registered the forces affecting the cube's surfaces, transferred them onto a 1 cm surface relief, and then milled them into five high-resolution formwork matrices.

The surfaces loaded with spatial information radically altered the interior space of the seven-tonne cube. The surface relief extended across all corners of the floor, walls, and ceiling. At first glance, it seemed that there were visual fractures in the pattern. Yet closer inspection revealed that these were actually a 90° change in direction of the mapped surfaces in the field of the imaginary force. The wall surfaces became receptors that—like computer tomography—displayed something that is normally invisible. A dialogue was created between the continuous, procedural space of the force field and the Cartesian geometry of the cube.

The algorithmically designed interior is distinguished by its surprising haptic qualities. The unexpectedly soft appearance of the concrete stands out against with the raw world of pre-fabricated construction and its ordered, exterior aesthetics. The surface relief alleviates the weight of the concrete elements, and the turbulent ripple pattern suggests softness and depth. The synthetically generated surface contours seem to be in constant movement. Few visitors could resist touching this strange new material.

This design paradigm, which can be transferred to complex, spatial geometries at different scales, is fundamentally different from conventional methods of applying patterns to architectural volumes. It allows us to distribute differentiated, three-dimensional information in virtual space and condense it, by means of digital fabrication, into physical, architectural elements.

At 2,883 m above sea level, a new mountain hut is being built for the Swiss Alpine Club. The timber construction is an applied research project of the ETH Zurich, and will use new building technologies in an exemplary way. In the restaurant area, the traditional decorative wood carvings will be interpreted in a novel way, using digital design and fabrication methods. Computer-controlled joinery machines have long been standard in the timber industry. These machines crosscut individual planks and beams at the correct angle, and cut slits and bore the necessary holes for assembly. Via "digital wood-carvings," which are transmitted to the machine as additional fabrication data, we extend this work step and exploit the full potential of digital fabrication with timber. The ornamentation covers the complete wooden structure and ceiling. Its continuous line pattern interprets the restaurant's spatial features as well as the material wood, into which the ornamentation is carved. Force fields that are defined in virtual space are mapped as lines on the physical surfaces that delimit the interior space. In this way the carvings combine innovation and tradition into a sensual spatial experience.

SUPERWOOD

WOOD CARVINGS, RESTAURANT OF THE MONTE ROSA ALPINE HUT, 2008–2009
In cooperation with: Studio Monte Rosa, ETH Zurich. Client: Swiss Alpine Club SAC

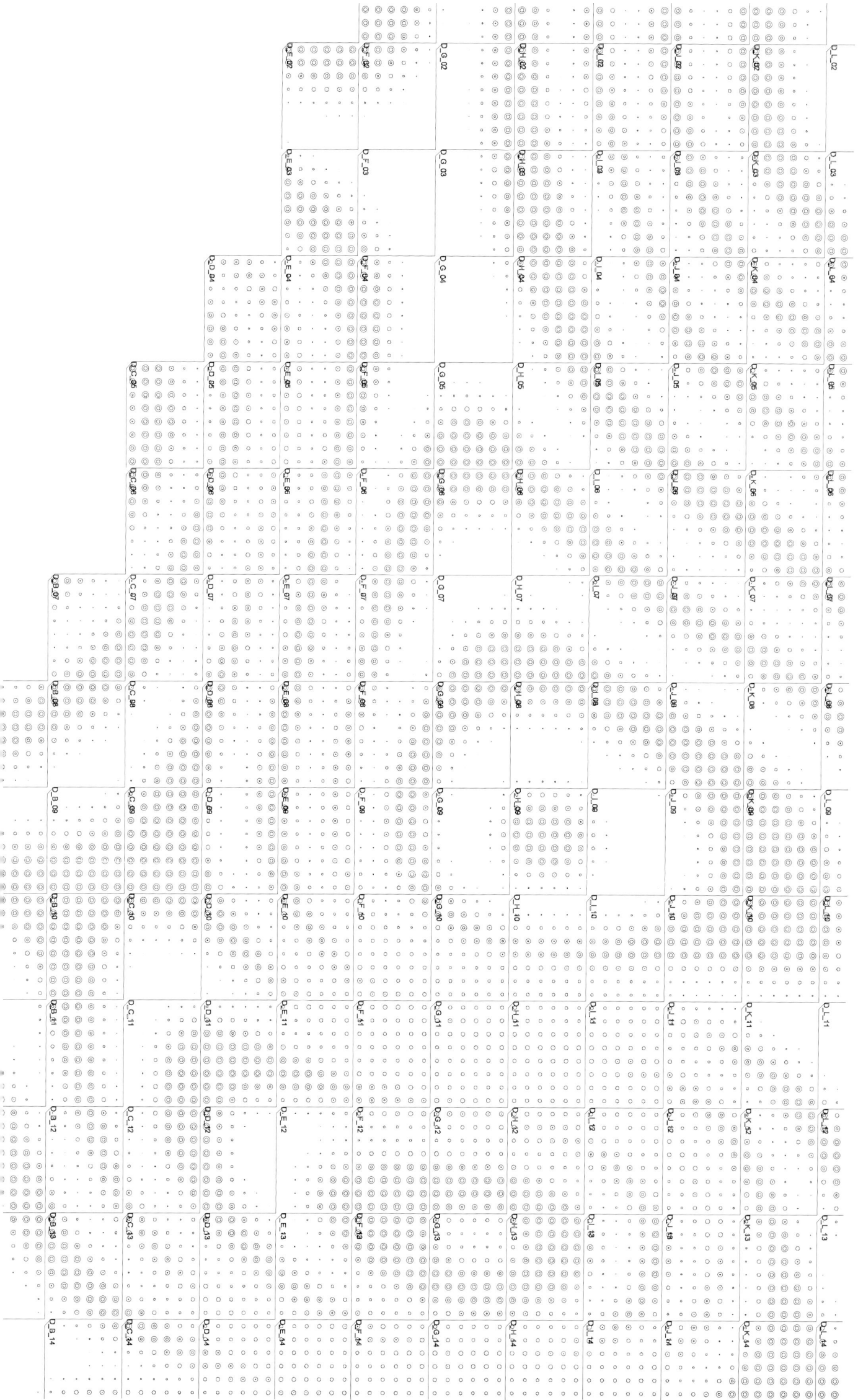

UNDER MY SKIN

SWISH*, EXHIBITION PAVILION AT EXPO.02, BIEL, 2000–2002
Clients: IBM and Swiss Re

ACOUSTIC PERFORATIONS. Instead of attaching acoustic panels to dampen reverberation in the exhibition space, we decided to perforate the wood-based ceiling panels, which meant we could expose the underlying insulating material to use it as an acoustic absorber. We designed these perforations as a sort of functional ornament; a 1000 m² ceiling pattern, which folded down over the walls in soft, flowing lines.

Milling the perforations conventionally would have exceeded the budget, because programming the CNC milling machine would have added costs for each and every one of the 400 ceiling panels. To realize our idea, we bypassed the traditional interface between architect and contractor by generating the milling data for the 2 × 1.5 m panels directly from our design sketches. The contractor no longer needed to process our data and could pass one panel after another straight through the milling tool. This reduced the price per square meter to a fraction of the original cost, including the work we invested in programming. To optimize the processing time for the 16,250 holes further, we designed a flared mill bit that could drill holes of varying diameters using a simple, vertical drilling movement: the deeper the hole, the greater its diameter.

The sWISH* Pavilion, which we designed for the Swiss National Exhibition, was home to an exhibition about the Swiss population's wishes. It was located at the far end of the artificial platform built over the lake for the Expo in Biel. The design of the 700 m² exhibition pavilion merges two initially contrasting ideas: an introverted, windowless black box that would nevertheless be "soft" and inviting. We decided to interpret the pavilion's whole exterior as one continuous, homogenous shell, made from a literally soft material: black polyurethane.

To generate a social space on the exterior of the pavilion as an extra part of the infrastructure, generous, inviting benches were carved out of two façades. Ergonomically shaped from molded plywood, the benches were set into the building's outer wall like negative reliefs. Their hard, light-colored material provided a strong visual and physical contrast to the building's soft, black exterior skin, which visitors could press to make an imprint. The building's tactile skin and the invitation to relax "in the façade," while observing the comings and goings around them, allowed visitors to experience the pavilion, without necessarily visiting the exhibition itself. The visitors were absorbed into the façade, becoming part of its image.

Inside the mysterious black box, the generous exhibition space was arranged around several openings in the floor that revealed the lake below. The perforations in this "sixth façade" gave vibrant life to this unusual and impressive room, extending the exhibition out into the space between the platform and the water's surface. At the same time, these openings allowed cool air to enter the exhibition space through them, and, along with the water-cooled roof, created a natural air-conditioning system that ensured pleasant interior temperatures.

The temporary nature of an exhibition pavilion allowed us to push the constructive experiment to the limit and build a structure where the combination of unusual materials and digital construction processes created a highly sensual architectural experience and conferred a strong identity on the pavilion.

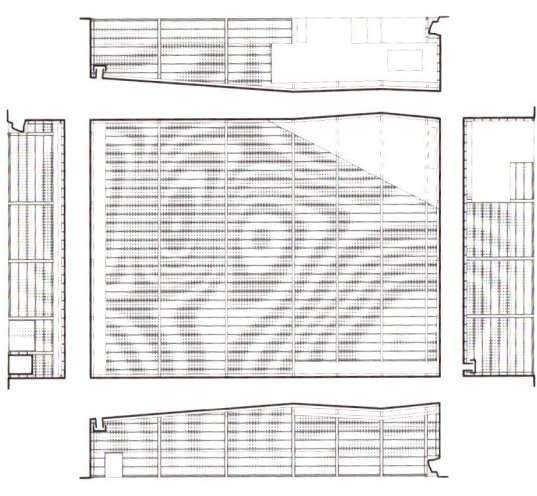

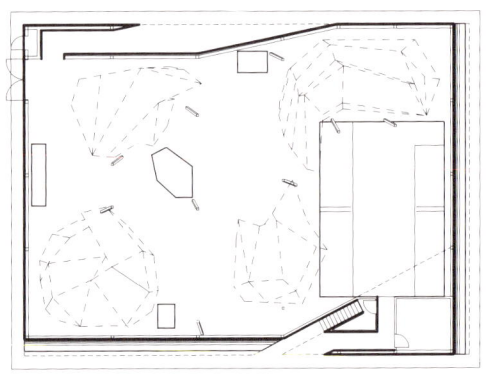

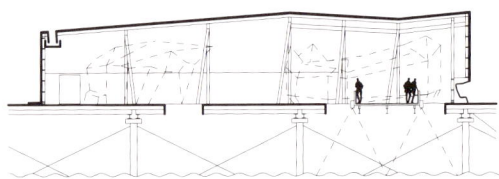

POLYURETHANE FAÇADES. A black skin made of polyurethane was stretched over the whole building. We sprayed the liquid plastic, which is commonly used for weather-proofing, as a sealing layer over the roof and walls, right down to the floor. We did not have to worry about the usual details such as roof edges, drains and corners, as the polyurethane created one continuous surface.

Using prototypes, we discovered that the amazing elasticity of the polyurethane even meant we could use the softness of the insulation layer directly beneath it to produce a tactile experience. This was fascinating. The layer of plastic thus genuinely became a skin, giving the building an unexpected and surprising physicality.

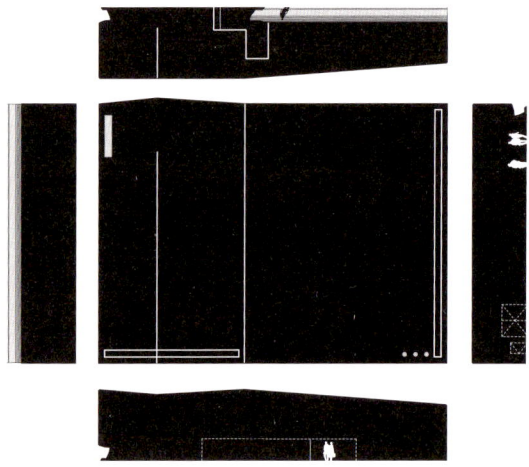

VEILING

PRIVATE HOUSE, RIEDIKON, 2004–2009

This dwelling, which reinterprets the typology of the surrounding gable-roof houses, gains its marked design by adapting form to context parametrically. The stipulations of two geometric operations were used to determine the groundplan shape of the house. One condition was to keep the neighboring house's view of the lake free; the other was to permit access and parking behind the house. Like a tent, an overhanging pitched roof covers the high rooms in the upper storey. The window strip, which runs along the edge of the roof, emphasizes the buildings volumetry. 315 vertical wooden slats, affixed to the surface of the wall, completely envelope the façades. By milling the edges, the cross sections of the slats were modulated in correspondence with the window strip so that requirements of sight and sun protection were fulfilled, and various, flowing levels of transparency could be set.

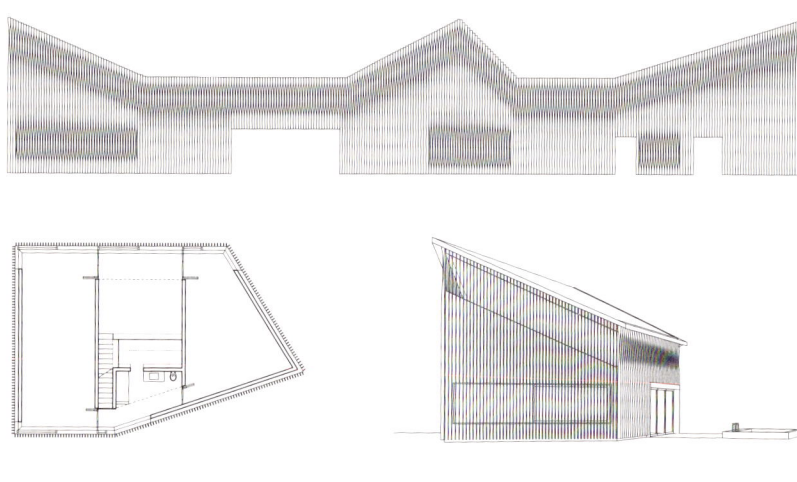

Interjections I

After twelve years of splines and parametrics, formZ-ided forms and X-treme formalizations, it seems crucial to start to pose some questions to the international community of designers in general, and to Gramazio & Kohler in particular. With their work, it appears that the digitalization of architectural conception will address not only issues of representation and conception, but also of fabrication. Here, the digitalization of architecture goes through a double process: design and construction. For a theoretician, the important issue being raised here leads to a series of queries:

1. Are we actually overcoming the Aristotelian conception of designing forms, that of "hylemorphism": from the Greek hylè (wood, or matter) and morphè (form)? Thought of as an active form (morphè) imposed on a passive matter (hylè), it is a concept that is at the root of several established oppositions, such as structure and ornament.

2. Are we observing a mutation of the meaning of two traditional approaches, already described by Gottfried Semper during the nineteenth century, that of Gemäuer (masonry) and Gezimmer (carpentry)?

3. And lastly, will these experiments in full-scale prototyping be able to displace the limits between Rohbau and Ausbau—a traditional opposition in German-speaking building culture?* It is understood that, by Rohbau, one refers to permanent structures, while, by Ausbau, one defines the fitting-out of architecture and the laying-out of equipment and devices. In other words, by blurring the differences, will those experiments lead to the vast field of interactivity? GEORGES TEYSSOT

* Laurent Stalder, The Persistence of the Ephemeral, Colloquium Rohbau versus Ausbau: Constructive Concepts of the Future, presentation, Department of Architecture, ETH Zurich, June 8, 2007.

This book is about a series of very elegant and convincing demonstrations of the potential of new technologies. So for me the questions are to do with how far each of these technologies can be pushed. What are the next steps in each process and what other processes are there which lend themselves to this 1:1 prototyping? With the mTABLE for example, there are two technologies involved: design from a mobile phone—so how far can that be pushed? Design a car? A house? A city?—and remote CNC fabrication—and so how far can that be pushed? Full size house printing? Control of a whole CNC factory?

The ultimate scenario is interaction with the whole planetary ecosystem from a mobile phone (or whatever replaces them). A nice first step would be to implement a version of Fuller's World Game on a mobile phone with Google Earth so that everyone could play the World Game and try to save the planet (1:1) whilst waiting for the bus... JOHN FRAZER

Could you explain which software you use and how you use it? BERNARD CACHE

To what extent can the shift that is occurring in other contexts also be seen to be working in Switzerland? What I can detect elsewhere has been a marked shift away from the scenography of postmodernism—using the term in its broadest cultural sense to include even deconstructivism—towards a new interest in performance and material processes. It is not as though appearance is unimportant. Rather questions of structure and material behavior can no longer be divorced so easily from ornament and aesthetics. And this shift, of course, is facilitated in an era of "digital tectonics" by digital performance modeling techniques and digitized forms of production. It is further reinforced at a theoretical level by an interest in the work of Manuel Delanda and new scientific thinkers. To what extent, then, can any similar shift be detected in Switzerland—a country that has been dominated for so long by an aesthetic of the box? NEIL LEACH

Are computational techniques in combination with fabrication the beginning of a new craft?

The spread of computational literacy in the realm of architectural design combined with computer numerical controlled (CNC) machines has opened up different approaches to design generation and implementation. Some examples for this trend focus on scaling up previously prohibitively complex processes and exploit digital technology for problem solving. Other approaches stand out for introducing genuinely new aesthetics by combining generative processes with new methods of fabrication.

These tangible products are made possible by generative processes that defy traditional product-focused evaluation, and they require different skills. On the one hand, such skills necessary to write custom programs still are a deterrent for many designers. However, progress is being made in teaching, and more accessible programming languages and environments for design are being developed. On the other hand, the hardware itself poses a problem. Similar to computers in the 1990s, the cost of today's fabrication equipment (especially at larger scales) is still prohibitive to many schools and private practices. But direct interaction with these machines is crucial in fostering a playful approach to learning how to use them and ultimately in expanding their fields of application. Similar to computer hardware, fabrication hardware is gradually becoming more accessible as well.

The challenge is to define new usage scenarios from the combination of generative processes and digital fabrication, the integration of material and assembly knowledge, and the development of a sense of aesthetics within this combined medium. To me, it is of less interest to use this technology to merely solve problems of complexity in construction that were previously impossible to build. Rather, the appropriation of the techniques should lead to a new form of craft; one that encourages externalizing of knowledge and sharing of experience and skills across disciplines, and enlarges our notion of tools to incorporate the digital and its information in novel ways into physical objects and encourage the continued development of technique. Form giving is only one aspect, its natural extension is the development of systems with sensing and behavior. AXEL KILIAN

DIFFERENCE VS. REPETITION
It has been suggested that with the advent of digital fabrication greater significance will be attributed to the notion of difference—as opposed to repetition—within building construction. Whereas prefabrication in architecture was driven by relentless reiterations of the same, deployed time and time again, to the point of total monotony, one now argues that computer-integrated manufacturing will liberate designers from the straitjacket of absolute uniformity. However, what seems to currently emerge within the field is a tendency to relegate difference to the domain of surface appearances, to subtle manipulations of decorative layers, and to the effect of spectacular form—to the point of indifference.* Where do you stand on the question of difference and repetition? How does your work diverge from prevalent tendencies? Or, to turn the query around, even from the point of view of conundrums, the question "what difference is there?" may always be transformed into: "What resemblance is there?"** MARC ANGÉLIL

* This is most likely not what Gilles Deleuze implied in Difference and Repetition when stipulating that works—whether literary or architectural—be "capable of affecting the mind outside of all representation." See: Gilles Deleuze, Difference and Repetition [1968]. Translated by Paul Patton, New York, 1994, p. 8.
** ibid., p. 12.

ON/OFF

TANZHAUS, CONTEMPORARY DANCE HOUSE, ZURICH, 2005–2007
In cooperation with: blue architects. Client: City of Zurich

ACOUSTIC SKY. 1,350 cubes of melamine foam adorn the ceiling and provide basic acoustic absorption; their reserved presence contributes to the character of the dance space. We treated the roof's soffit and sidewalls as one continuous surface and arranged the cubes in upward-arching lines. The serial arrangement of the lines smoothes out the difference between the wall and the ceiling surface so that the room is consolidated as an entity. To the observer, a dialogue is set up between Robert Maillart's filigree concrete truss structure and the new curved, coarse-grained lines.

Because the roof had to be reconstructed, we were able to integrate a low-tech method, projecting the digital design information directly onto the actual ceiling elements, into the prefabrication process. We projected our CAD plans from a laptop, via a projector, straight onto the prefabricated elements. The carpenter simply applied a cube-sized double-sided adhesive to the projected markers, element by element, marking the position of the cubes precisely. After the elements were installed in the construction, all we had to do was remove a protective film from the cubes and stick them to the adhesive.

Changes in use had transformed the former electricity substation structurally and formally several times in its 100-year history. Recently we converted it into a center for contemporary dance. A few strategic interventions into the existing structure have given the raw, industrial building a new identity. The project uncovers and emphasizes its existing qualities; the new interventions are superimposed on traces of the former substation and accentuate the building's raw charm. New and old combine to play a game of deception.

In sunlight, the building's silver mineral paintwork and large windows reflect the colors of its surroundings. During the day, new, flush-mounted windows accentuate the existing volume, allowing light deep into the interior of the building and revealing its new spaciousness. By night, artificial lighting emphasizes the building's interior, the plasticity of the façade becomes evident, and the deep reveals make the building's solidity both visible and physically tangible.

Inside, we created generous spaces and concentrated all the secondary rooms in the unlit central zone. The core of the design is the dance space: 400 m² without pillars, and 11 m high, it was created by removing a floor that had been inserted after the original construction. The imposing, exposed roof structure of filigree concrete trusses, which formally resembles a wooden construction, is an early work by the engineer Robert Maillart. New acoustic absorbers are arranged in a wave-like formation that draws attention to the studio's ceiling. The ten square windows make strong spatial reference to the surrounding urban landscape with its tall trees, and transmit a sense of spaciousness.

The dance studio can also take on a second, completely different character. A simple but sophisticated system of folding, two-tone interior shutters allows the room to be transformed into a blacked-out, totally sealed, anthracite-colored space. In this sealed-off state, the deep window recesses become colored light boxes, projecting the dance space onto the façade and revealing the interior's activities to the outside world.

FOLDING SHUTTERS. The dance studio can take on two different characters. To light the dance performances, the room must be completely darkened. By contrast, during the day the generous window openings flood the room with natural light and make it an ideal rehearsal space. A happy coincidence helped us here: we discovered that, inside the dance studio, the ratio of windows to wall surface was exactly 1:1. This allowed us to develop a blackout system of folding shutters that would solve the switch between those two contradictory requirements.

The two-tone internal shutters can be folded out from the center of the room; when they are open, their surfaces form a continuous white band, 3 m high, interrupted periodically by the glass window surfaces. The shutters are no longer recognizable as such and create a light-colored visual horizon that expands the room into a landscape. However, when the shutters are closed, the room is transformed into an anthracite-colored, smooth-surfaced performance space. The eye is no longer drawn to the light band of windows and the exterior, but toward the spacious room and the generous ceiling area.

This simple and self-evident structural solution, which was inspired by the pre-existing façade, allowed us to turn contradictory demands into a spatial quality. The room takes on different characters, depending on whether the window shutters are open or closed.

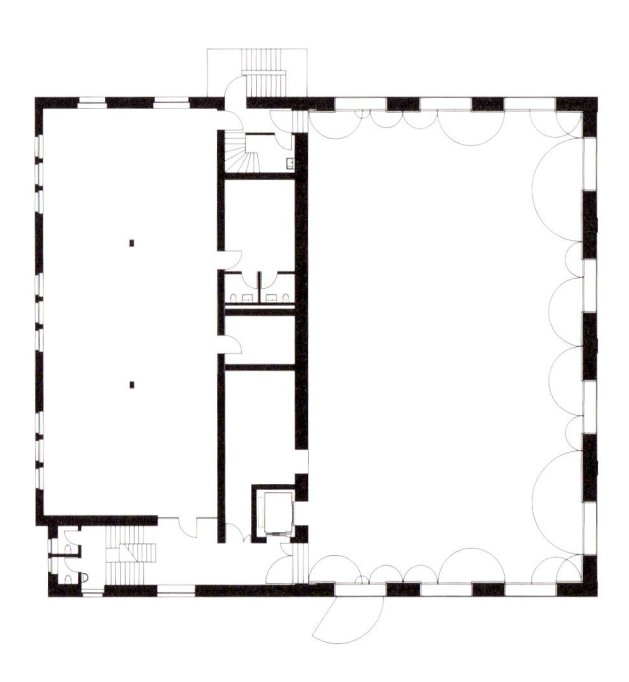

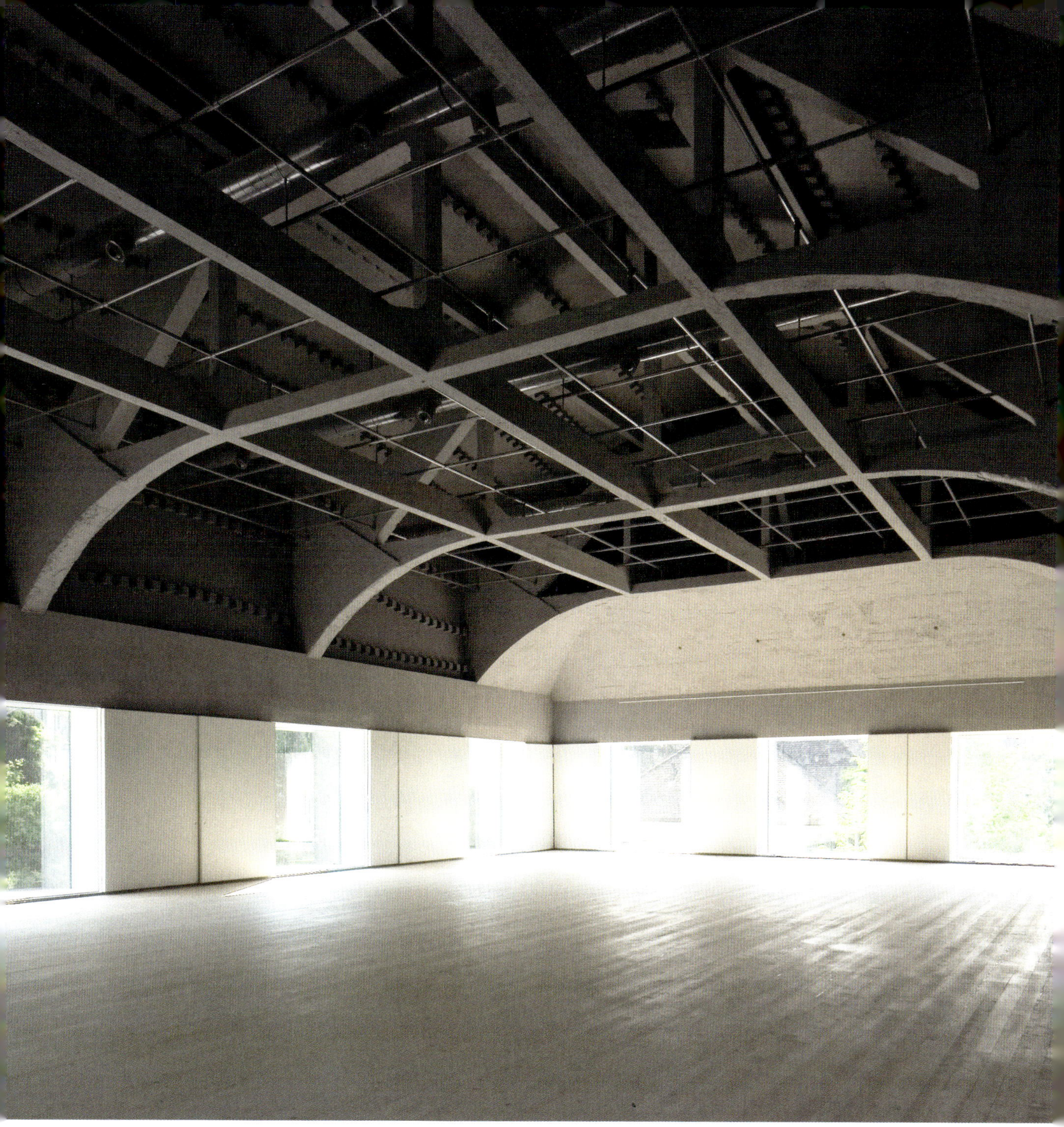

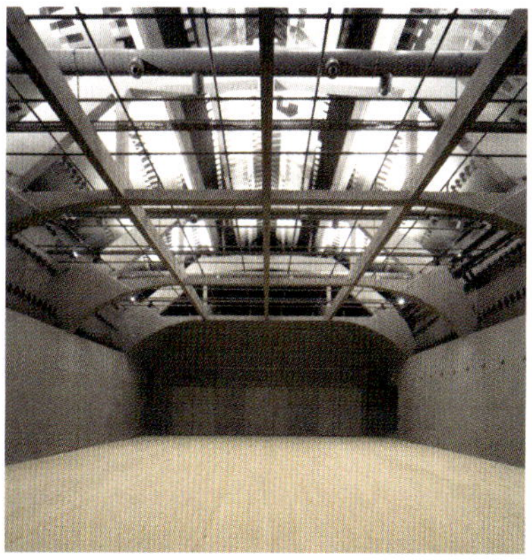

GLOWING FRAMES. In the silver painted façades LED bars are inserted into the reveals to transform the ten windows by night into colorful, glowing volumes. These "glowing windows" delineate the first-floor dance studio on the three façades, giving it an active presence in the nighttime city.

The design principle we established for this sensual light installation in the façade actively involves the users of the Tanzhaus. Directors can select the color of the light for the evening on which their piece is performed. The color modifies the appearance of the house and establishes a link to the dance performances inside it. As the system does not allow dynamic changes in color, a single defined color has to be chosen for the evening. We imposed this restriction to ensure that the color selection would be made consciously and thus be personal and meaningful. If there is no performance on a given evening, the light boxes glow mutely.

The façade with its glowing windows is an architectural information system that uses simple means to great effect. It transports the activities inside the building to the outside, and extends the building's interface with its urban surroundings.

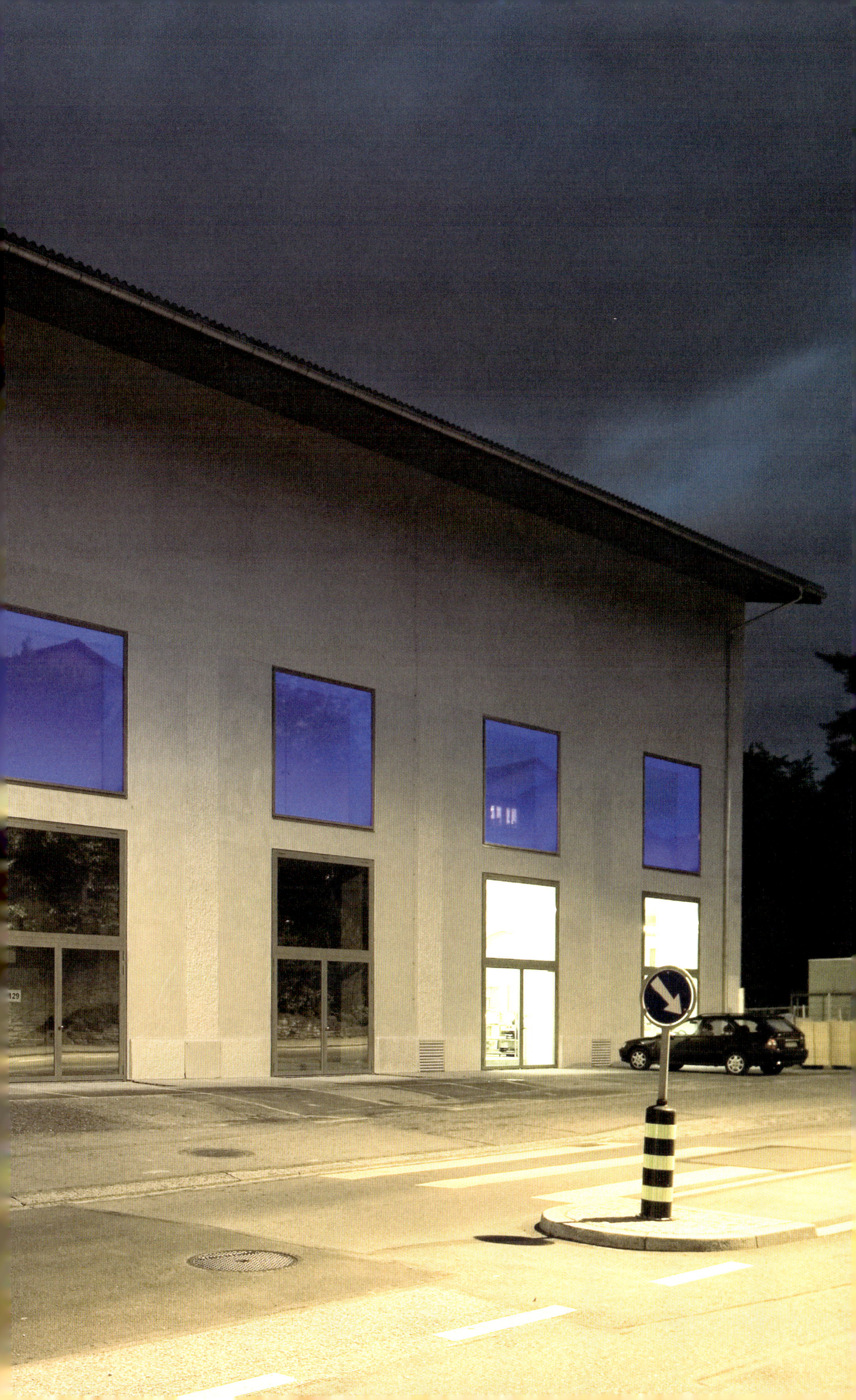
129

LIGHTLINE
POLYCHROME LIGHT INSTALLATION, USTER, 2006–2008
Client: City of Uster

At night, the lights—barely visible by day and embedded in the road surface—stand out in a zigzag line. Slowly flowing changes of intensity and color enliven the installation, which is monochrome to trichrome according to the season, and gives the city crossroads a marked identity. Artificial light is used here not as a static medium, but as a dynamic one.

The possibility of smoothly adapting its brightness and color to functional and aesthetic requirements that vary over time provides diverse potential for designing the public space and its night-time qualities. This means the light can unfold a "behavior," which helps to generate a specific urban identity. In view of such extended properties, we consider light to be a fascinating building material and a contemporary means of design in urban planning.

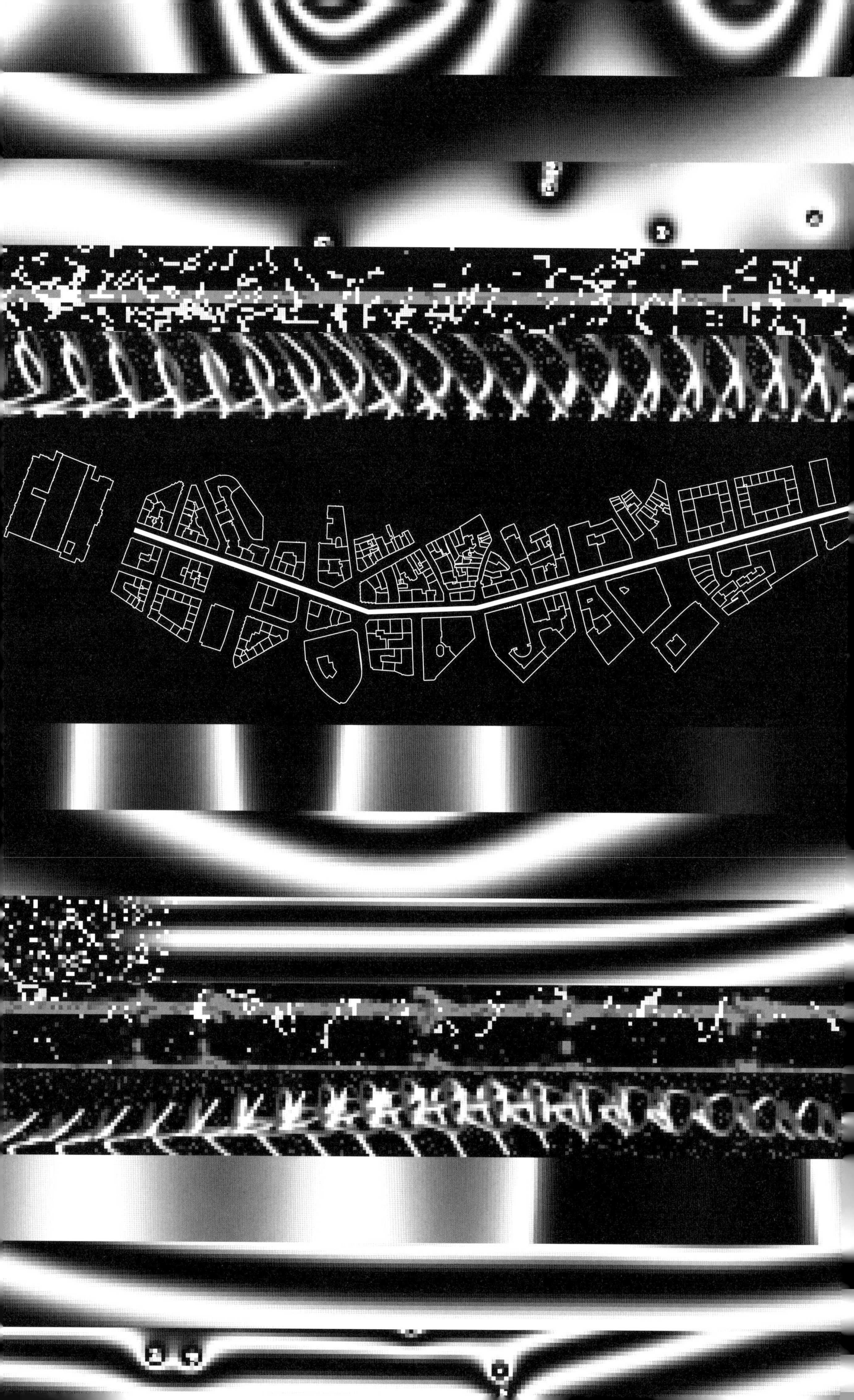

THE WORLD'S LARGEST TIMEPIECE

BAHNHOFSTRASSE CHRISTMAS LIGHTS, ZURICH, 2003–2005
Client: Zurich's Bahnhofstrasse Association and Zurich Municipal Electric Utility

XMAS GENERATOR. During the Christmas season the Bahnhofstrasse is illuminated for eight hours every night, with a constant flow of changing light sequences. Designing this 320-hour urban environment was an innovative, exciting and demanding task that stretched the classic architectural repertoire to include the algorithmic design of time-based sequences.

Thus the lights are "played" by custom software that controls the 8,800 LED bulbs in real time. We designed the parameters and rules of the algorithm to be potentially unlimited. The installation's distinctive identity is conferred by the constant creation of new, unpredictable light patterns. Movement sensors affect the design and reflect what is going on below. But the Christmas lighting responds to people on the street gently and quietly, without overemphasizing its interactivity.

"Distinctive, generous, unique"—these were some of the qualities expected of the Christmas illuminations in Zurich's internationally renowned shopping street. The competition brief also called for an interpretation that was contemporary in both aesthetic and technological terms. We designed a continuous band of lights, 1.1 km long, using 275 tubes of light, which we called "The World's Largest Timepiece."

In terms of urban planning, the installation connects the railway station to the lake. Its simple, linear course turns the band of light into the visual backbone of the city, accentuating the appearance of the Bahnhofstrasse and its two slight yet distinct changes in direction. The vertical rods down the middle of the street form a spatial contrast with the building façades to each side, and draw the onlooker's gaze upwards into the night sky. Depending on where the observer is standing, the Christmas lighting can look like a slick series of individually lit tubes, or like a glowing, constantly shifting curtain of light.

It is the nature of light to be dynamic, not static. Modern digital technology for controlling light intensity means that light can now be used as a highly flexible, informative medium. The appearance of the Christmas illuminations evolves dynamically over the course of Advent and creates a constantly changing atmosphere of festivity. The pattern shown on the band of lights is generated by an algorithm regulated by date as the festive season progresses, as well as by the street's activities, which we record using sensors. Hence, the visual image reflects not only the passage of time, but also the life of the Bahnhofstrasse itself. The passersby influence the lighting patterns in a sort of collective interaction: the Christmas lighting becomes the city's inner timepiece and creates an unpredictable, dynamic and disembodied architecture, as transient as clouds in the sky.

LIGHT TUBES. The 7 m high tubes had to provide light evenly in all directions, and be able to withstand heavy windloads despite being light in weight. We therefore had to find a rigid, robust casing material that would also transmit light.

Eventually we chose wound glass fiber technology: a special manufacturing process in which glass fibers are soaked in resin and spun around a mandrel. We were fascinated by the additive logic of this process. The winder controls the stacking of the fibers via two computer-coordinated movements. A sliding carriage drives the glass fibers back and forth along the spinning mandrel, creating an extremely stable multi-layered tube. The stacking winder and the number of tiers and overlappings determine the rod's flexural rigidity and torsional stiffness, as well as its transmission of light.

The bands of glass fibers are wound into a rhomboidal structure: the thick areas provide structural stability, and the slender necks create optical brilliance. We used software that simulated the fabrication process and several physical prototypes to achieve the optimum combination of light diffusion and structural rigidity, testing effective optical qualities such as brilliance and surface structure under both night and day conditions.

The final tube was 7 m long and 15 cm in diameter, but its shell was only 2 mm thick; including the lighting and control technology, it weighed just under 23 kg. Intense engagement with the computer-operated production process allowed us to integrate two normally incongruent requirements into a single material, thus using wound glass fibers for lighting on this scale for the first time.

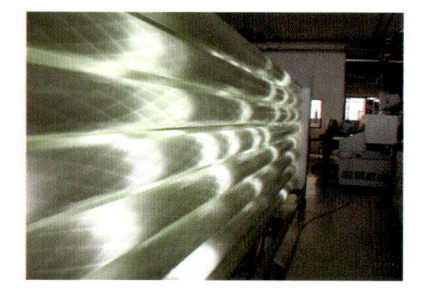

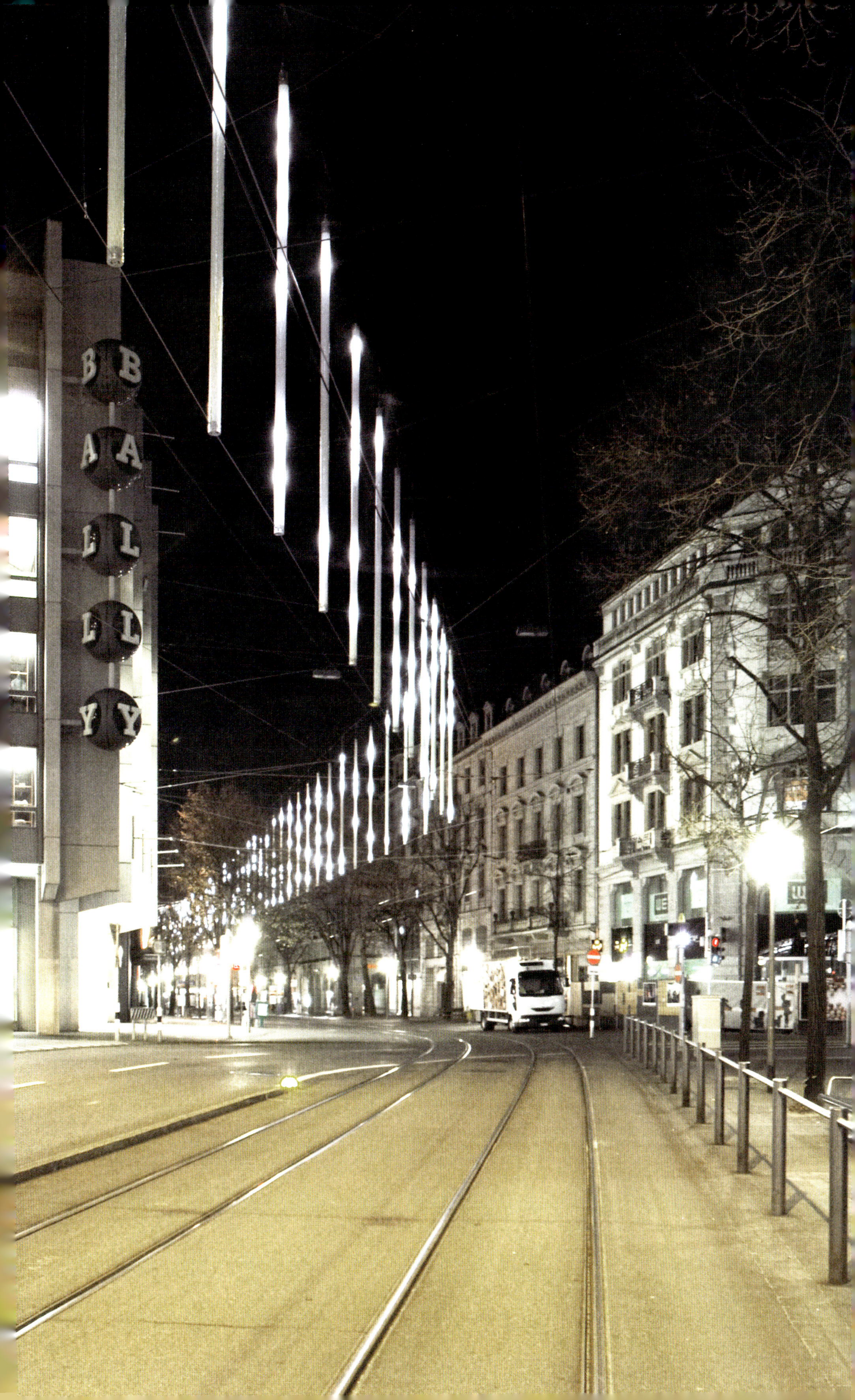
BALLY

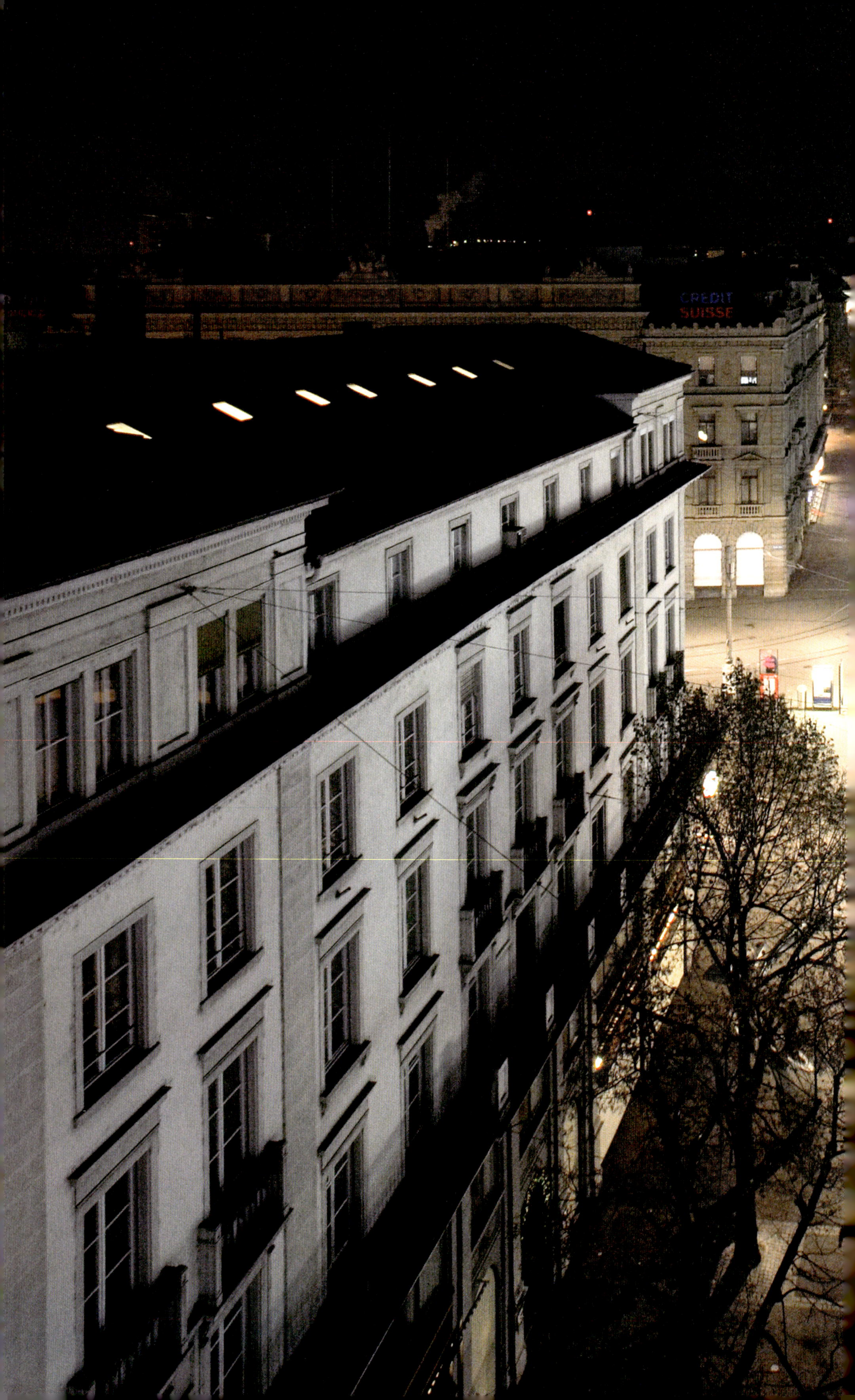
CREDIT
SUISSE

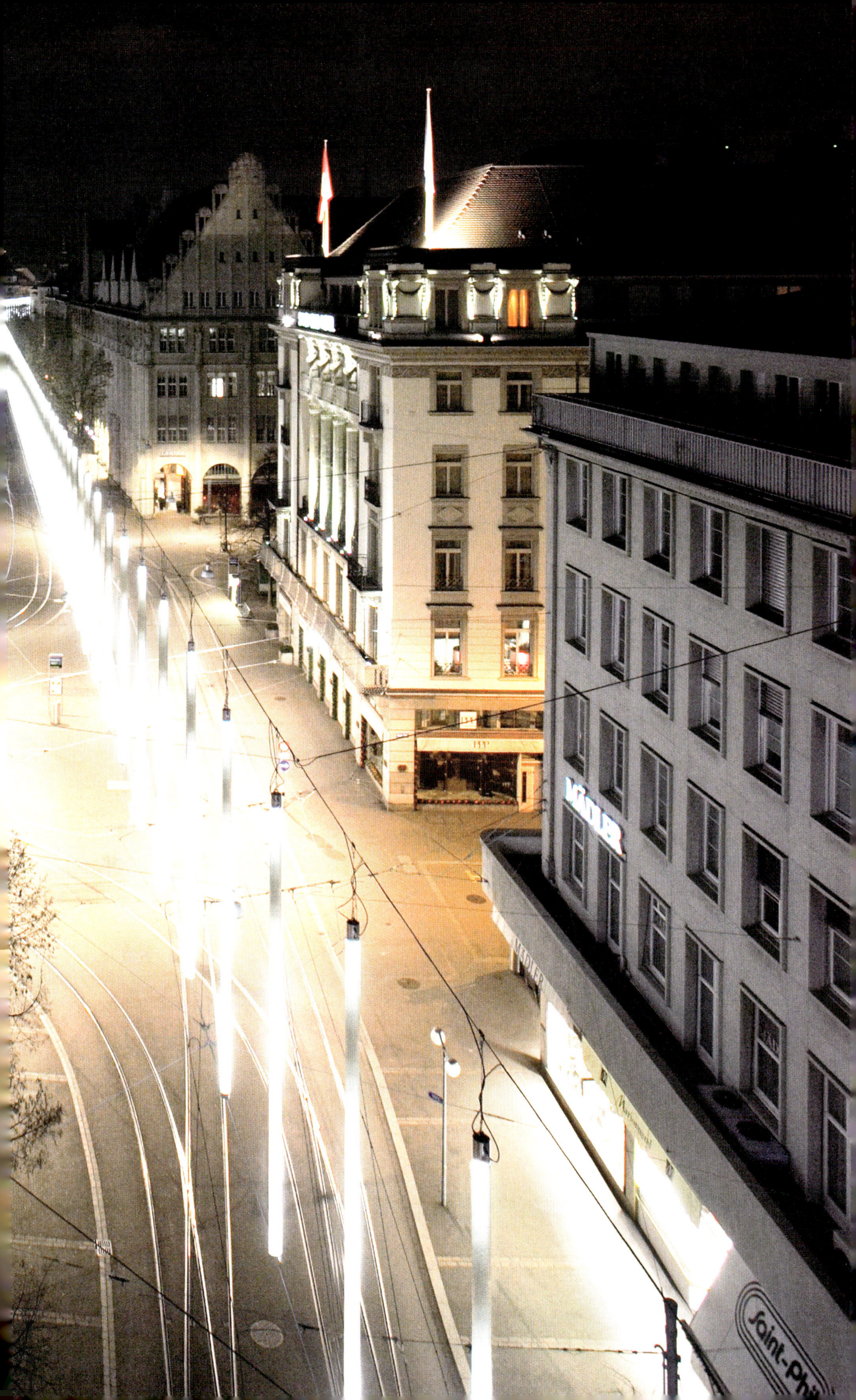
MÄDLER

DFAB ROBOT CELL, ETH Zurich, 2005. This research facility offers the possibility of processing building elements of up to 7 by 3 m at a scale of 1:1, using a variety of tools specified by the architects themselves.

A Short Biography of KR150 L110

Brenda Lynn Edgar

KR150 L110 is an industrial robotic arm equipped with 6 axes, each controlled by an electromechanical drive system with brushless AC servomotors.[1] Classified by the International Federation of Robotics as an "articulated robot,"[2] KR150 L110 can lift up to 110 kg and perform just about any automated task; from palletizing and de-palletizing banana crates to welding and painting cars, and as we've recently seen, laying bricks. It can even do all that upside down, mounted on the ceiling. It comes from Augsburg, Germany, where it was manufactured by the KUKA robotics company. The one used by Gramazio & Kohler is one of the 126,700 robots that were installed worldwide in 2005, excluding those used in the defense industry, the figures for which are not published.[3]

KR150 L110 is also orange; RAL color reference 2003, or "security orange". Used as KUKA's standard color, "security orange" stands out against any background, reminding us that this complex piece of heavy machinery is not particularly observant of misplaced hands or feet and requires caution when operating. "Security orange" is also a color that has become synonymous with a globalised world that is progressively dominated by automation; in fact, it is often employed by contemporary artists to evoke just that. The image of a bright orange industrial robot is readily associated with an aseptic factory environment devoid of any human presence that might hinder its Stakhanovic production rate—a metallic incarnation of Karel Capek's nightmare vision, that he baptized "robot" in 1920.[4]

Fortunately, at Zurich's Federal Institute of Technology (ETH), the robotic arm finds itself in an entirely different setting and has been given an entirely new function. The robot laboratory of the chair for Architecture and Digital Fabrication is installed in hangar C51 of ETH's Building, Environmental and Geography department—an enormous hall littered with various geotechnical experiments, concrete mixers, piles of bricks and wood, cranes etc. In the midst of all this, poised in a pristine white metal and glass box, KR150 L110 appears as a rather incongruous element, like some sort of Dadaist sculpture—a comparison that is perhaps not too far from the truth. The robot is an integral part of industrialized building processes which for better or for worse have dominated post World War II architectural production. But in Gramazio & Kohler's digital fabrication lab, the robot has been extracted from the monotonous world of mass production. Instead of repetitively stamping, cutting, welding, or moving, the robot performs multiple and varied tasks to create highly unique and carefully crafted

---

1 A "servomechanism" is an automatic control device; they are commonly used for the control systems of guided missiles, aircraft, and manufacturing machinery. "Servomechanism", Columbia Electronic Encyclopedia, *Reference.com* http://www.reference.com/browse/columbia/servomec, August 3, 2007.

2 There are six types of industrial robots: Cartesian/Gantry, Cylindrical, Spherical, SCARA, Articulated, and Parallel (*http://www.ifr.org*, August 1, 2007).

3 *http://www.ifr.org*, August 1, 2007.

4 The word "robot", derived from Czech robota meaning hard or forced labor, was first used in Karel Capek's theatrical piece entitled *R.U.R.: Rossum's Universal Robots* (Prague, 1921), first performed in 1920. It has been said that Capek himself credited the invention of the word to his brother, painter and writer Joseph Capek (*http://capek.misto.cz/francais/robot.html*, August 1, 2007).

World Business 15 Feb 2002 p

The New York Times

Adding the Android Touch

Hiroyuki Yoshino, left, the president of the Honda Motor Company of Japan, and Richard Grasso, the chairman of the New York Stock Exchange, with Asimo, a Honda robot. Asimo became the ... ever to open the Big Board yesterday, wh... anniversary of Honda's listing was comm...

Robocrop
A Cut through the Visual History of Robotics 1921–2028
Jules Spinatsch

objects. In true Dadaist spirit, Gramazio & Kohler have transformed the industrial robotic arm (an as-found artifact) by giving it a new context (the architectural design studio) and a new function (the craftsman's tool).

But what kind of "robot" is KR150 L110? Is it the kind that makes ice cubes or the kind that dreams of electronic sheep? Where does it fit in the history of robots that have populated myths, artistic creations and industrial production since the dawn of civilization? An abundance of science-fiction literature and films, scientific writings, historiographies, technical manuals and treatises offers definitions for the term "robot" that are as numerous as they are ambiguous. Nonetheless, as IT engineer and author Cyril Fiévet observes, these all share the following characteristics: 1. The notion of movement, measured in terms of "degrees of freedom", where each degree is controlled by a motor (the human arm, for instance, is equipped with seven degrees of liberty, not including the hand); and 2. The mimetic notion, which can be identified throughout time, as most inventors of machines sought to reproduce human or animal functions. Fiévet proposes the following definition: "An artificial creature, most often mechanical, autonomous or not, capable of moving itself partially or entirely and performing specific tasks, and which takes on either human or animal characteristics in varying degrees."[5] KR150 L110 clearly meets these criteria: it operates with up to 350° of freedom, is equipped with numerous appendages or "hands," and is commonly referred to as an "arm." It would be safe to assume that it does not belong to either the science fiction or mythical creature family of robots (such as androids or Golem figures), which are more of a reflection of the human being's bi-millennial desire to create life in his own image. While it may be a by-product of research in artificial intelligence, KR150 L110 is not a machine destined to recreate life or human intelligence. Incapable of speaking or making even the most rudimentary decisions, it is not what one would call an "intelligent" machine at all. Like all modern industrial robots, it is more akin to the automaton—the two terms being in fact synonymous.[6] Historically however, creators of automatons from Ancient Egypt and Greece to 18th century European watchmakers and those of today's robotic "pets" have consciously adopted human or animal forms (the artifice of these objects often being an integral part of their magical effects).[7]

The lineage of KR150 L110 would sooner be found somewhere between that of industrial robots and the computer itself. The very first industrial robot manufacturer, Unimation, was founded in the United States (Connecticut) in 1956, in the wake the staggering advancements in electrical and mechanical engineering brought about by the developments of the first computers in the 1940s.[8] Founded by two engineers, George C. Devol and Joseph F. Engelberger, Unimation built their first industrial robot in 1958. The Unimate, as it was called, consisted of an electronically controlled telescopic arm equipped with a "hand." Its commercial début was in the factory of General Motors in 1961, where it was used to move heavy cast metal pieces.[9] But the PC control of the robotic arm, which would provide its ultimate advantage over other robots, was made possible by advances in Computer Aided Manufacturing (CAM) software. CAM was

---

[5] Cyril Fiévet, Les Robots, Paris 2002, pp. 9–10. Author's translation.
[6] "Robot", Columbia Electronic Encyclopedia, Reference.com http://www.reference.com/browse/columbia/robot, August 2, 2007.
[7] Philippe Breton, A l'image de l'homme: du Golem aux créatures virtuelles, Paris 1995, p. 80.
[8] The development of computers was a truly interdisciplinary enterprise made possible by teams of mathematicians, physicists and electrical engineers. For a fascinating account of these pioneers of the early years of computing, see: Mike Haley, Electronic Brains, Washington D.C. 2005.
[9] Chantal Leguay, Les Robots: une histoire de la robotique, Paris 2005, p. 30.

developed after the first experiments with Computer Numeric Controlled (CNC) machines. One such machine, The Whirlwind, was developed at MIT's Servo-mechanism laboratory between 1945 and 1951. Initially developed to respond to real-time inputs, the Whirlwind was connected to an industrial milling machine in order to make complex mechanical aircraft components for the United States Air Force starting in 1951. The startling potential that this presented gave rise in 1955 to the creation of an entirely new programming language called APT,[10] which would ultimately enable CAM to be combined with CNC machines in the 1970s. Unfortunately for architecture, the building industry changes much slower than the US military does and CNC machines would have to wait until the late 1990s to even begin being incorporated into schools and professional practices. Advances in technology and increasingly user-friendly CAM software have since made CNC machines available to a larger public. Milling machines, laser cutters and even 3D printers are already common features in the model shops of architecture and design schools—at least in the industrialized world.

It would be incorrect, however, to situate KR150 L110 in the lineage of CNC Machines, which are typically task specific. Whereas one robotic arm can perform all subtractive and additive processes with a wide variety of materials (milling, cutting, bending, stacking, spraying etc.), a different CNC machine would be necessary for each task. To its disadvantage, KR150 L110 was not conceived to be as "user friendly" as a CNC machine; its size, supporting infrastructure and programming demands make it far too cumbersome. It is also very dangerous: assembly lines comprised of robotic arms are often isolated in order to protect human workers, and safety development is an important area of research in the robot industry. This makes its application at the ETH all the more unique, where it is used much like a universal craftsman's tool to make one-off architectural elements, most of the time with custom written software. The robot lab itself, affectionately referred to as "the cage," resembles more of an open experimental workshop than an assembly line. Students fearlessly wander in and out of "the cage," feeding the robot cement blocks and breathlessly watching their creations materialize before their eyes.

Thanks to the willingness of Swiss brick manufacturer Keller AG to experiment with new applications of the robot, KR150 L110 will soon travel to construction sites in the form of a mobile robot lab called "R-O-B"; a specially equipped shipping container from which the robot will operate in order to ensure safety as well as deal with things like construction dust and uncontrollable weather conditions. It would seem that the industrial assembly-line robot is not quite adapted to personal fabrication or on-site interventions. It might have to go through one more generation of cross-breeding with another kind of machine called a "service robot." Designed to function in the company of humans, the service robot is defined as one that "operates semi or fully autonomously to perform services useful to the wellbeing of humans and equipment, excluding manufacturing operations."[11] This is rather interesting if we consider that architecture at its best is generally useful to the wellbeing of humans and, at its worse, an automatic assembly of prefabricated parts.

After the Arts and Crafts movement in the nineteenth century, the architectural and design collectives that flourished in the early twentieth century such

---

10 Neil Gershenfeld, *Fab. The Coming Revolution on Your Desktop—From Personal Computers to Personal Fabrication*, New York 2005, p. 40.

11 "Service robots: Definition", *http://www.ifr.org*, August 3, 2007. They are used in a wide range of applications, from surgery to washing aeroplanes. The Japanese service robot "Mighty Hand" is even used on construction sites to lift heavy elements, such as concrete panels, into place.

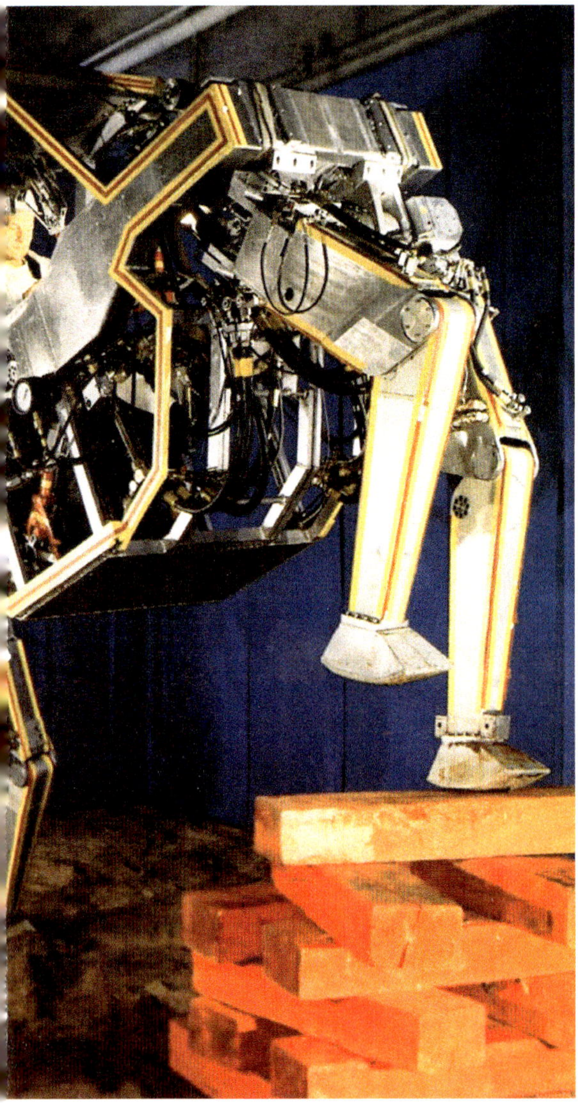

MOBOT

LIVE
AL GORE NEW VP!
ASIMO
ELECTORAL ★ VOTES
270 NEEDED
ASIMO 267
BUSH IV 3
CNN
★AMERICA VOTES 2028★
12:10p PT
AMERICA ELECTS FIRST ROBOTIC PRESIDENT!
Worth1000.com

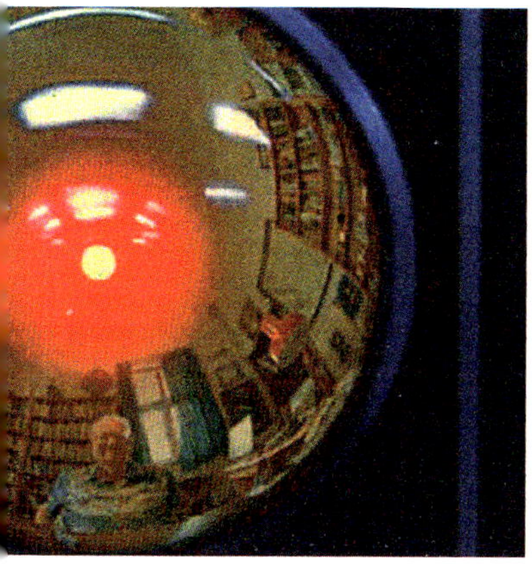

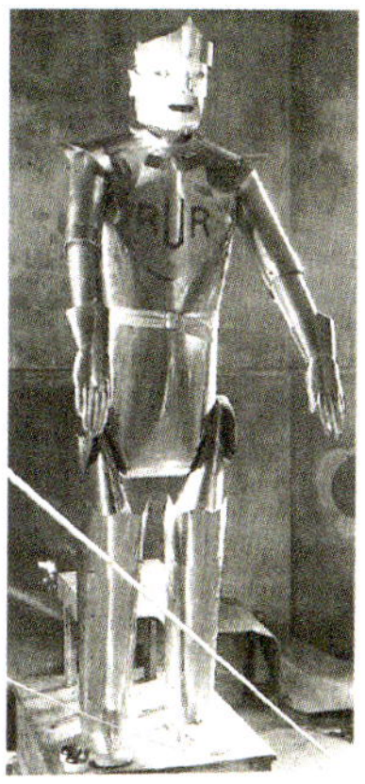
RUR

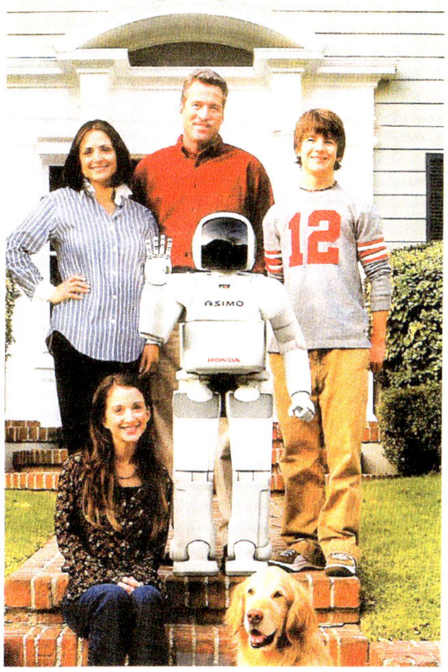
12
ASIMO
HONDA

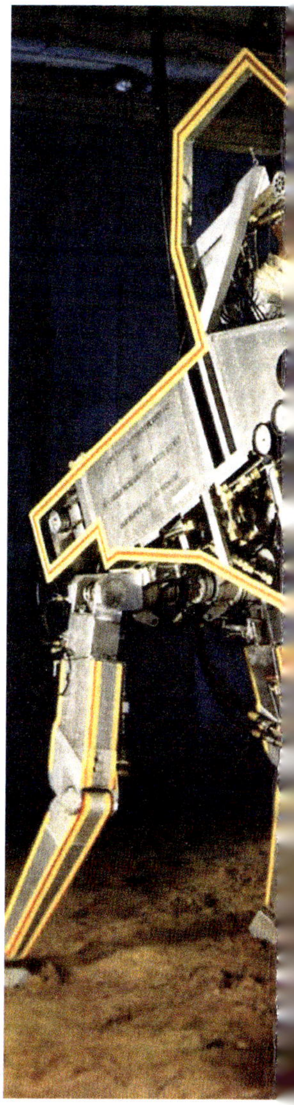

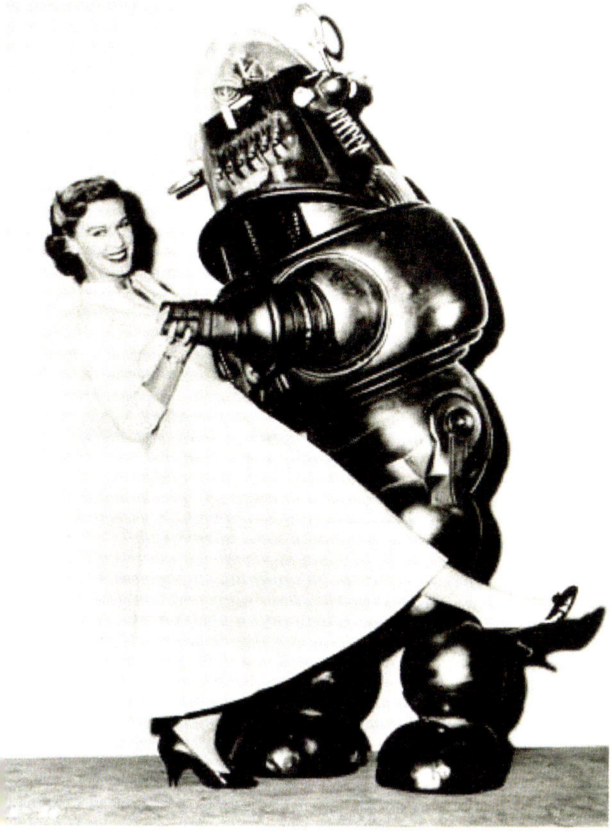

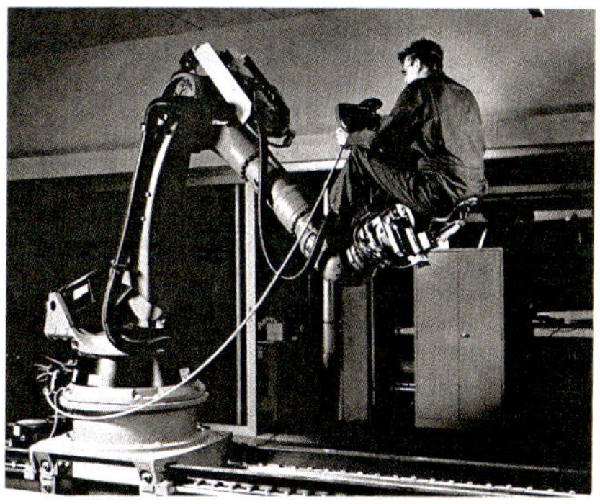

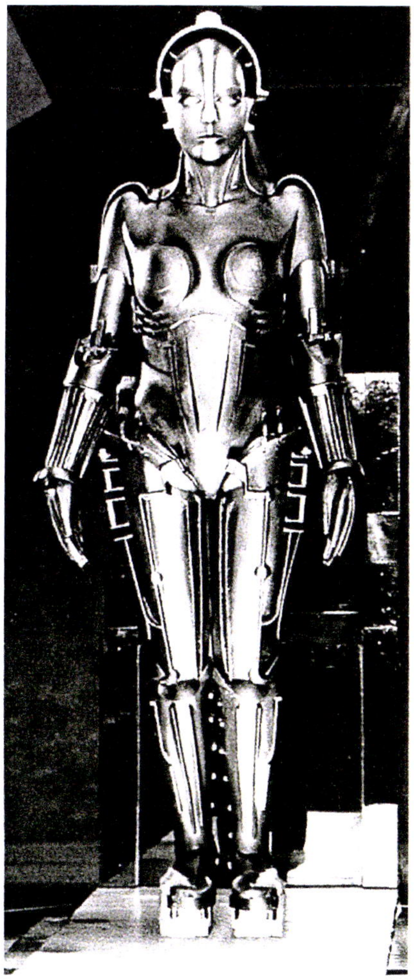

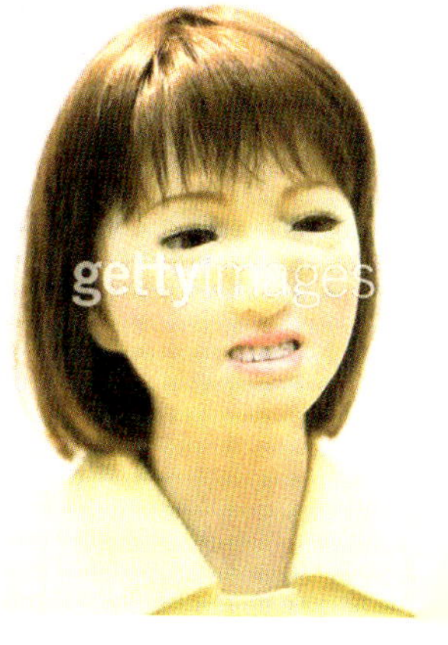
gettyimages

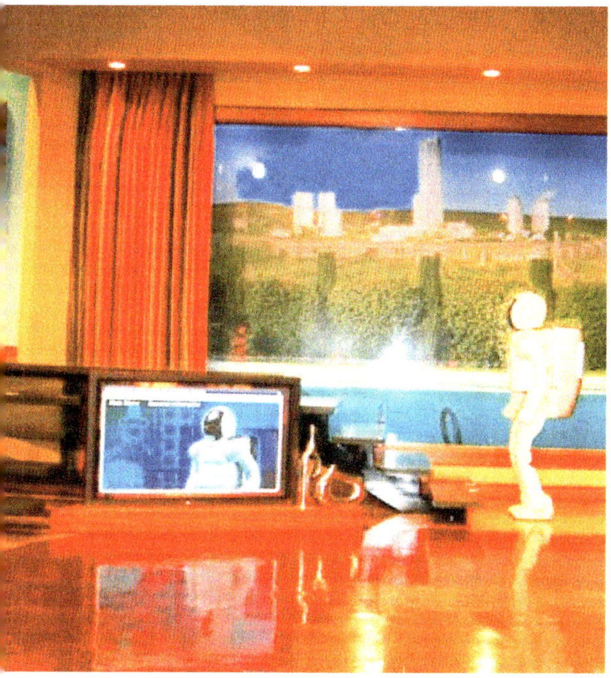

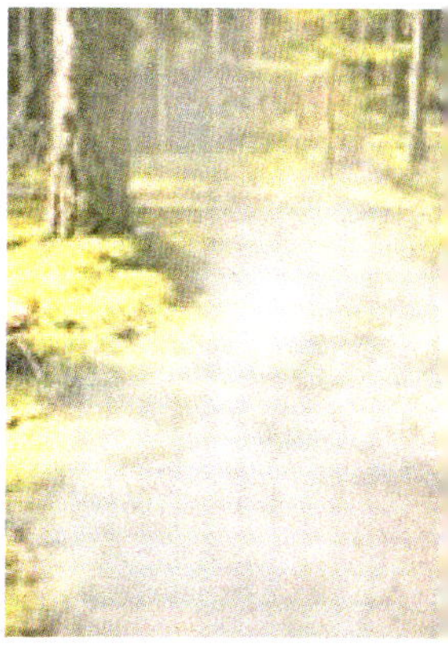

as the Wiener Werkstätte (1903), the Deutscher Werkbund (1907) or the Bauhaus (1919) all sought to reconcile fine craftsmanship and design with the methods of mechanical mass production brought by the industrial revolution. It is clear that in the early twenty-first century, architects must now reconcile their art with digital processes as well. However, while Gramazio and Kohler's experiments at the ETH are promising, perhaps the potential of KR150 L110 does not lie in the hands of architects alone. As Fernand Braudel reminded us, the value of any innovation is ultimately given by the social and political forces that sustain it and render it indispensable.[12] If projects to integrate robots into architecture are not to go the way of previous utopias or simply become more vectors of mass consumption, architects might wish to consider the social and political impetuses that could sustain such innovations.

12 Fernand Braudel, *Civilisation matérielle, économie et capitalisme, XVe—XVIIIe siècle*, Vol. I, Paris 1979, p. 378.

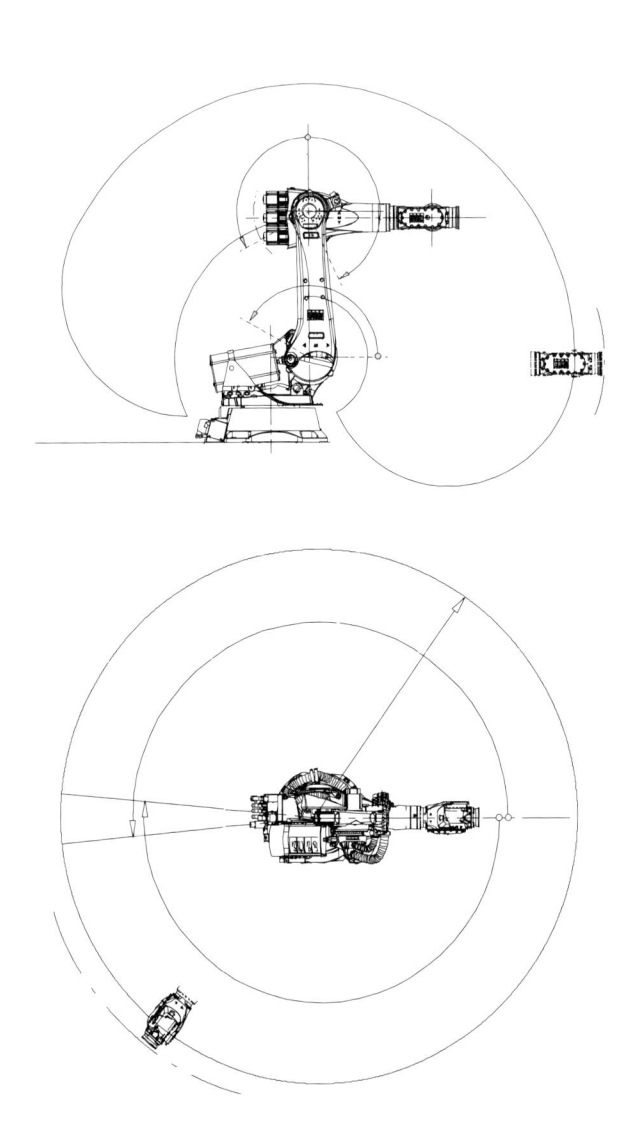

R-O-B

ROBOTIC FABRICATION UNIT, 2007–2008
In cooperation with: Keller Ziegeleien

R-O-B extends the traditional prefabrication process: the robot leaves the protected environment of the production hall and ventures out to the building site. Housed in a modified freight container, the R-O-B mobile fabrication unit can be used anywhere in the world. It combines the advantages of prefabrication—precision and consistent high quality—with the advantages of short transport routes and just-in-time production on the building site. Furthermore, the mobile fabrication unit is not restricted to a predefined manufacturing process or a particular building material. It can also produce highly varied, digitally described constructions using local materials.

Academic partner programs, workshops, and prototypical industrial applications will be used to collect, exchange, and disseminate experience of decentralised, robot-based architectural production. The primary assumption is not that R-O-B will construct a complete house, ready for occupation. Rather, the unit will be employed where it is able to play off its advantages over traditional building methods: in the manufacture of building elements with highly specific forms which can therefore only be designed and fabricated via computer methodologies and the use of computer-controlled machines.

Interjections II

D'Alembert once said: "Abuser de l'esprit philosophique, c'est en manquer." Could robotics lead us out of the impasse created by the abuse of philosophy in architecture? Could pure practice and know-how save architecture from fashionable criticism and fake moral?

To what extent can personal and light robotic equipment lead to lighter structures of production, lighter architecture and lighter urbanism on a global scale?

What about the political implications of robots? Peter Sloterdijk had the following suggestion: "If we managed to integrate the intelligent machines of the future into semi-personalized and semi-animist relations with humans, the prospect of man actually befriending the robot would be less alarming. The mission of our time is to develop a post-modern humor that enables cyberneticians to get along well with cardinals, mullahs, and voodoo priests."* PHILIPPE MOREL

* Peter Sloterdijk, Essai d'intoxication volontaire: conversation avec Carlos Oliveira, Paris, 1996.

"Marco Polo describes a bridge, stone by stone. 'But which is the stone that supports the bridge?' Kublai Khan asks. 'The bridge is not supported by one stone or another,' Marco answers, 'but by the line of the arch that they form.' Kublai Khan remains silent, reflecting. Then he adds: 'Why do you speak to me of the stones? It is only the arch that matters to me.' Polo answers: 'Without stones there is no arch.'"* LARS MÜLLER

* Italo Calvino, Invisible Cities, Translated from the Italian by William Weaver, San Diego, New York, London, 1974, p. 82.

The work of Gramazio & Kohler, and in particular their DFAB research at the ETH Zurich, is of extraordinary interest as it unfolds architectural qualities from a design approach that is of similarly ambivalent character as the main focus of their research: computationally controlled robotic manufacturing and construction processes. On the one hand these technologies, which are only now becoming more widely available in the construction industry after being employed in other fields for many years, are mainly used as merely facilitative means that may elaborate the formal repertoire of architecture but are essentially extensions of long established (and conventional) design methods and processes. On the other hand these technologies can provide an inroad to an alternative practice of architecture, one that rethinks top down design and engineering solutions from which they themselves originate. Being driven by truly generative, evolutionary processes they enable highly articulated material and construction systems, which in interaction with the luminous, acoustic and thermal environment, open up a tempo-spatial richness that requires a different skill set, sensitivity and intellectual approach to be comprehended and instrumentalized. How can designers embrace these opportunities and challenges as modes of (re)thinking architecture rather than just advancing the way we build?
ACHIM MENGES

Bachelor machines are very seldom conceived and developed to literally function as such. They are rather meant to introduce open scenarios, paranoia and frustration; a coitus interruptus that suggests other possible narrative and fictional procedures which could liberate the small arrangements of scientific and social dances from their alienation.

How legitimate would robotics be, with its parametric and programmable machines, if it confined itself to productive and constructional modes in the search for programming mechanisms and the authority of modernity? The contemporary scene is riddled with alienating subjectivities; why not face them and develop them as schizophrenic narratives that work simultaneously as an operational reality and the murmur of something that is happening at the moment, a vector of uncertainty and incompletion? Like A.M. Turing himself, between the computing power of Enigma and his suicide, Snow White version? FRANÇOIS ROCHE

WHAT WOULD KANT THINK?
He tells us that the sublime effect of an Egyptian pyramid comes not from its sheer size, but from our failure to comprehend the great number of blocks from which it is constructed. For maximum impact one must be neither too near nor too far: the whole must be visible, but each part must also be distinct. Based on this, Kant characterizes the sublime as a strictly quantitative experience.

With their intricate stacking of blocks, your programmed walls encourage the same middle-distance viewing, the same perceptual oscillation between part and whole. Their effect, though, is quite different: they offer not the overwhelming, negative pleasure of the sublime, but the playful, positive delight of the beautiful. Your programmed walls thus conflate the quantitative aspect of the Kantian sublime with the qualitative, formal pleasure of the Kantian beautiful. We are forced then to devise a new term to describe their effect: quantitative beauty. We trace their undulations like the ornamental patterns that Kant gives as exemplars of the beautiful, but we also see that they are assembled out of countless discrete units precisely positioned by a computational algorithm. Through technical means of production you create architectural forms that echo the engaging complexity of nature— a highly appropriate representation of our times.

Of course Kant also has very strict ideas about the proper place of beauty: its purposelessness, he argues, makes it inappropriate for any functional form, especially architecture. He writes that adding beautiful patterns to a serious building is like the superfluous tattooing of a body. What would you say about your new sort of beautiful forms? Have we learned to appreciate the purpose of architectural tattoos? SEAN KELLER

When I have the chance, I often like to watch your orange-colored industrial robot, which stands like a lonely, beautiful, caged alien animal. I always feel he is rather melancholy. As though he didn't know where to direct his power; as though he intended to do something, but wasn't clear exactly what. And questions often flit through my mind, which I would like to ask you now:
How much does one robot-hour cost?
How many breaks does he take?
What is his lifespan?
Have the students given him a nickname?
Do they tell him off?
Does he make mistakes?
Could he catch a mouse?
Could he function in the wild?
Are there more of his species?
PHILIP URSPRUNG

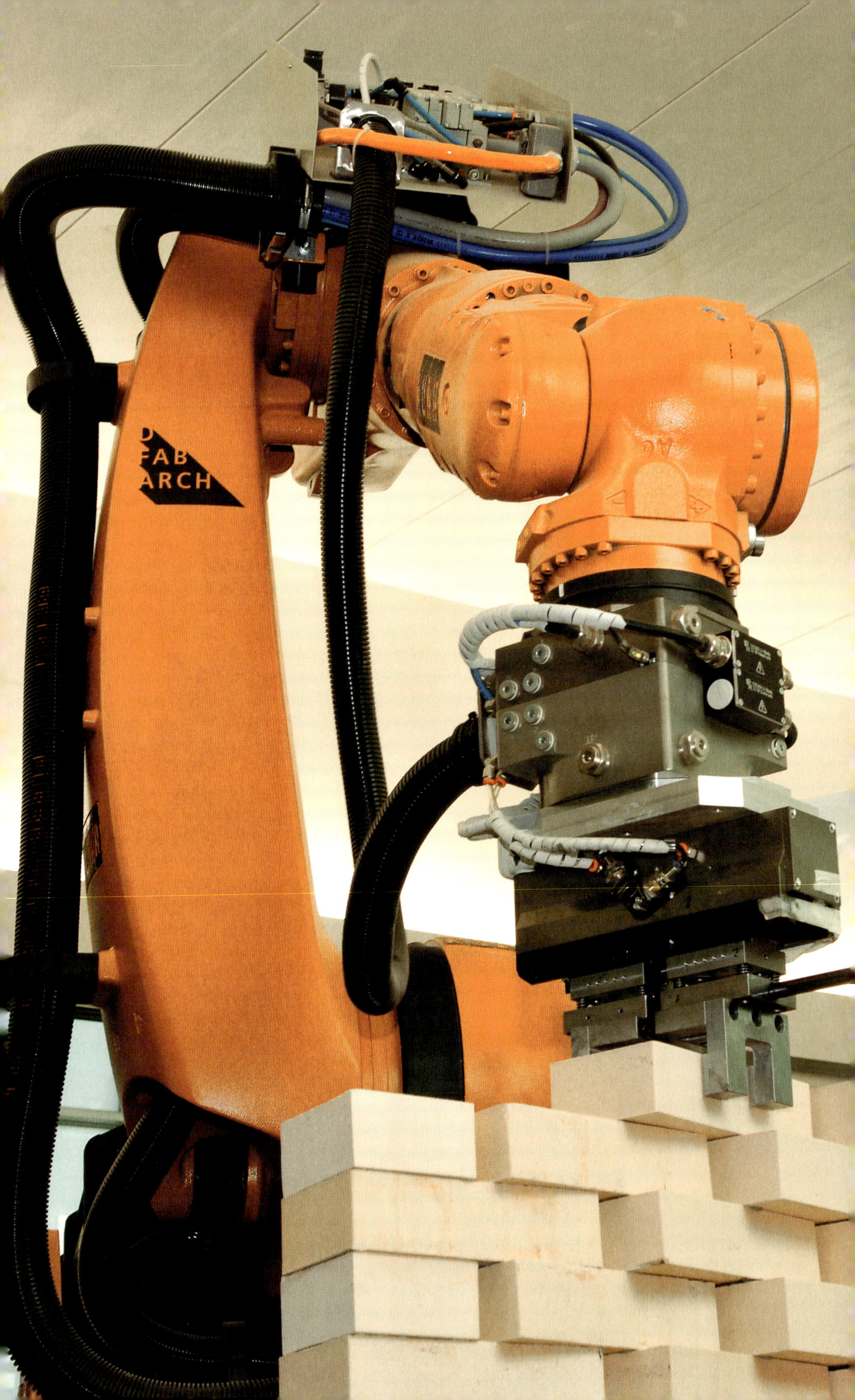
D
FAB
ARCH

ADDING ON
RESEARCH AND TEACHING PROJECTS ON ADDITIVE PROCESSES, ETH ZURICH

Architecture is largely made up of the addition of parts or the aggregation of materials into a greater, space-defining whole. The additive methods developed for this, simplified and transferred to the medium of digital fabrication, can be understood as a three-dimensional printing process. As we accumulate materials precisely at the point where they are needed, form and function are woven directly into building components; we are not limited to the design of their surfaces but can manipulate the entire cross-section of an element. Architecture is thus "informed" right down to the level of the material. The spectrum of building materials that can be processed additively ranges from rigid, geometrically defined modules such as bricks to fluid materials like concrete or foams.

We first tested out the constructive potential and architectural consequences of this approach by building brick wall elements. Through the continuous, procedurally controlled variation of position and rotation of individual bricks, fluid transitions between open and closed areas were created. The wall's structural patterns, plasticity and transparency changed dramatically depending on the incidence of light and observer's viewpoint. Some of the walls are deformed through the continuous projections and recessions of the bricks. Others appear from particular viewpoints to be strongly three-dimensional, although all the bricks lie at one level. The walls, which were designed in a digital, deterministic process and built by robot, are characterized both by the archaic presence of the material and by the differentiated properties of their procedural design. By enriching traditional and proven elements of the building industry with information, components are created that were hitherto unknown in this form.

The different properties, the variability in size and the plasticity of the materials we have so far used to build additively—bricks, autoclaved aerated concrete, wooden slats, and polyurethane foam applied in liquid form—have in each case decisively influenced the design logic and generated their own, usually unexpected but always fascinating aesthetic.

THE PROGRAMMED WALL, 2006–2007. If the basic manufacturing conditions of architecture shift from manual work to digital fabrication, what design potential is there for one of the oldest and most widespread architectural elements—the brick? Students investigated this question in a four-week workshop, designing brick walls to be fabricated by an industrial robot. Unlike a mason, the robot has the ability to position each individual brick in a different way without optical reference or measurement, i.e. without extra effort.

To exploit this potential, the students developed algorithmic designs that informed the bricks of their spatial disposition according to procedural logics. Positioning this way it was possible to draft a brick wall in which each of over 400 bricks took up a specific position and rotation in space. The students defined not the geometry of the wall, but the constructive logic according to which the material was organized in a particular temporal order, and which thus produced an architectonic form.

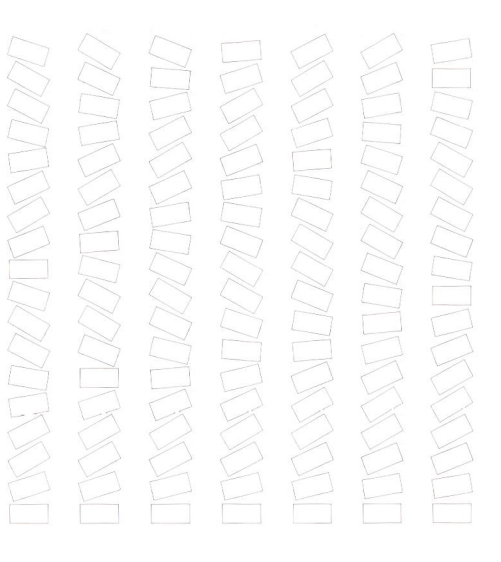

DOMOTERRA LOUNGE, Swissbau, Basel 2007. The wall was developed as part of a workshop for the Swiss Brick Industry Lounge at the Swiss building fair. The three-dimensionally formed geometry lends the element its stability.

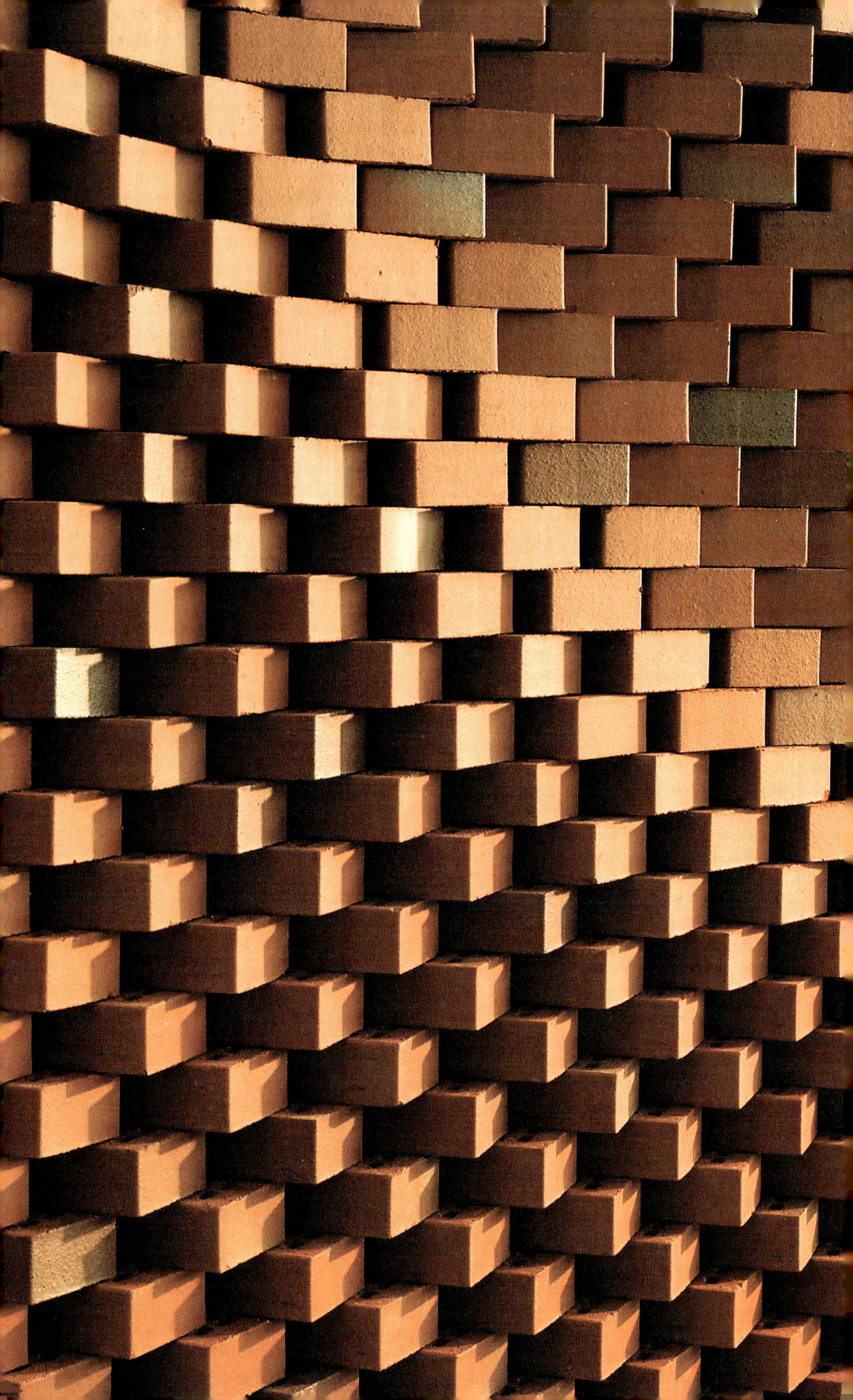

THE RESOLUTION WALL, 2007. In this project we investigated the additive construction of a wall made of autoclaved aerated concrete cubes of different sizes, their edge lengths varying from 5 to 40 cm. The time needed by the robot to put in place a module like this is independent of its size, because the required movement path remains the same. The use of large modules can therefore accelerate the building of a wall many times over, but reduces its resolution and thus the possible level of detailing on the surface and in the interior of the component. An intelligent distribution and jointing of different module sizes can resolve the conflict between the aesthetic and functional advantages of the finest resolution, and the economic necessity of the most efficient fabrication process.

Small modules can be placed where a high density of information is desired, while areas with low information density can be built quickly and efficiently using large modules. Since a change in resolution typically corresponds to a change of material, the combination of different module sizes in a homogenously materialized construction element has an unusual and stimulating effect. The joint pattern of the walls transmits a sense of the procedural design logic concealed within the depth of the material. Although the constructional complexity may be perceptible to the observer, it can no longer be completely decoded. The different modules meld into a new whole, the flat areas built of large blocks entering into a dialogue with the fine resolution and fragmentation of other areas. Sometimes these appear to gush forth from the depth of the elements, while elsewhere they resemble the result of an erosion process.

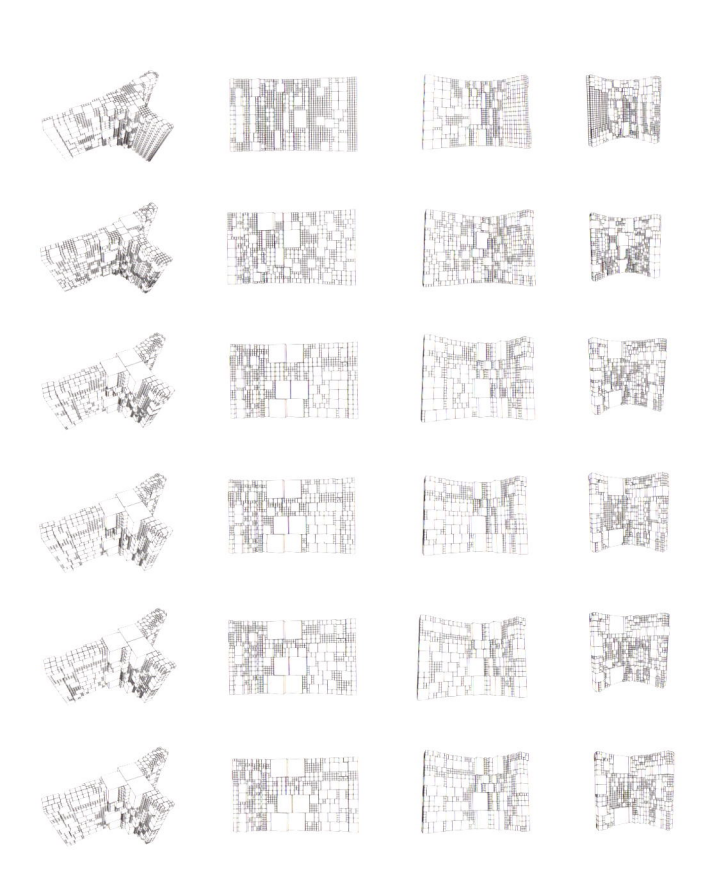

DISTRIBUTION. For the robot to be able to construct the wall prototypes on a scale of 1:1, we had to ensure that the block organization would be effective in terms of construction. Because of the large number of module combinations, we used a genetic algorithm. New generations of the system are generated from the overall system mutation. Only the generations that show greater fitness than their predecessors are used further. In our case, one condition of the optimization function was to use the modules with the largest possible dimensions, as this shortened fabrication time. The other condition was to achieve the greatest possible serration between the individual modules so that the overall construction would be stable.

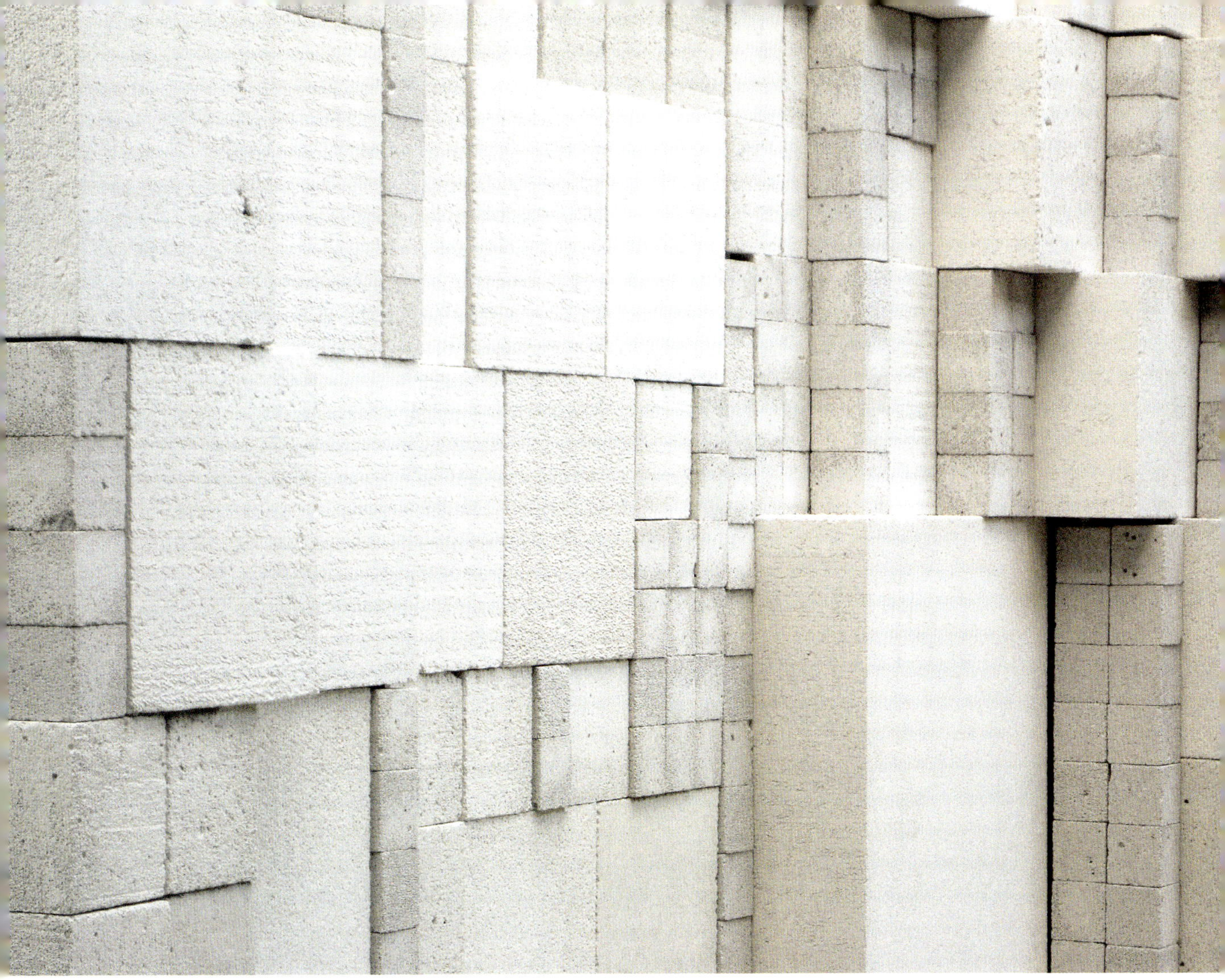

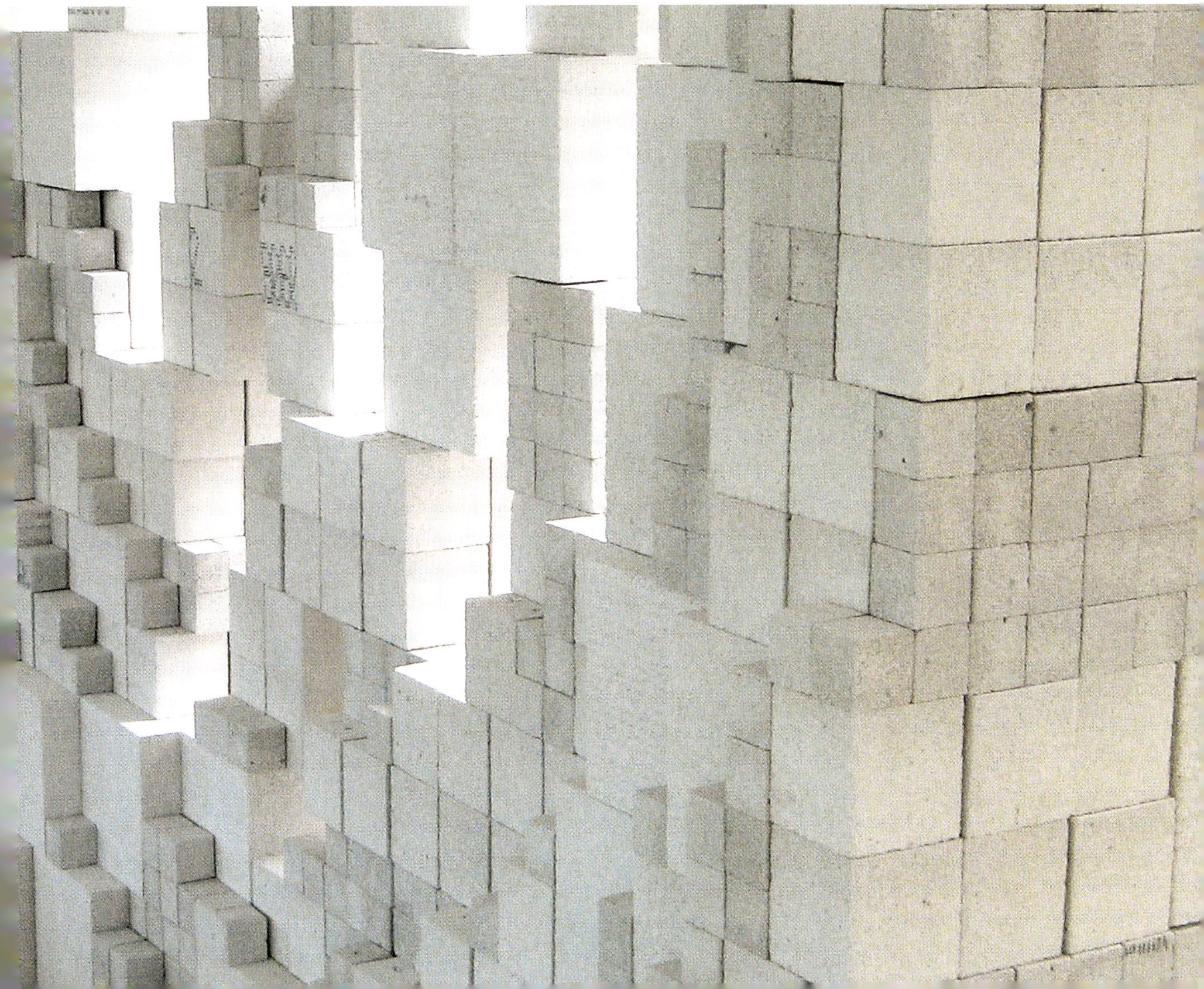

FOAM, 2007. When additive fabrication uses a material that is liquid, foams up and then solidifies over a period of time, the mutual dependency between the final shape, the paths of movement that control the robot and the intrinsic material properties can be grasped. In reality, the geometrical description of the foam layout constitutes only a small, insignificant fraction of the information needed for its production.

The fabrication process has two temporal components, which interlock and yet are offset from one another. In one part, the robot arm lays the liquid polyurethane foam along a path from start to end point. On the other hand, as soon as the foam emerges from the nozzle, a second process starts: after a few seconds the liquid material begins to react, and expands to many times its original volume, before it solidifies after about two minutes to take on its final form. The combination of these two movements — the first through space, the second through different physical states — means that when building up several layers, the morphology of the substructure is still in a state of transformation as new material is being added. Thus, a geometrically simple, almost banal grid can produce an astoundingly complex and formally multilayered artefact, provided it is foamed in a particular sequence and at a particular speed.

The layers of foam are not, as they appear, woven together like textiles, but rather they permeate one another. If, during the manufacturing process, the upper layer touches the lower while still liquid, they will flow into one another forming a homogenous node. But if the lower layer has already foamed and solidified, the added liquid foam will flow off to the side and generate a formally complex cross-over, tapering to its highest point. More challenging input geometries produce structures that are formally highly complex and, despite their apparently chaotic expression, technically reproducible.

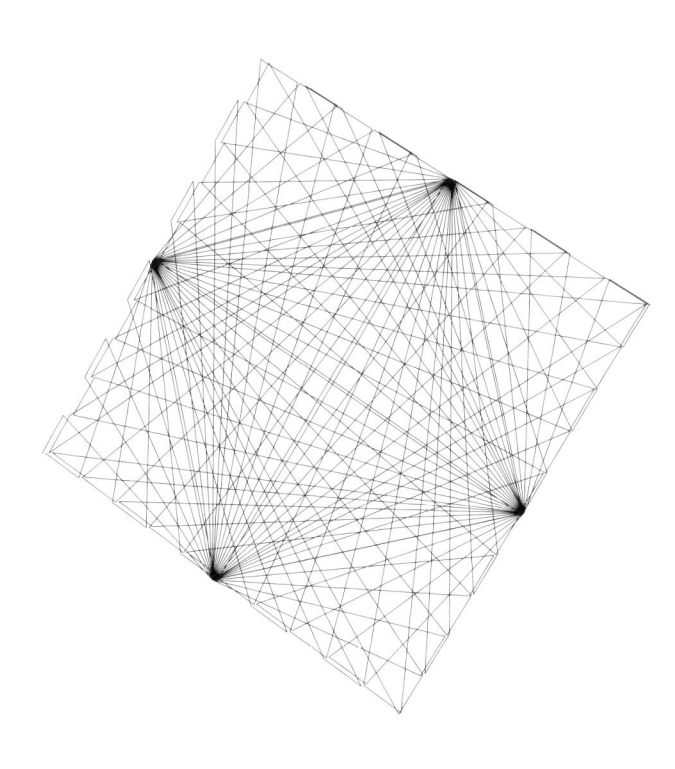

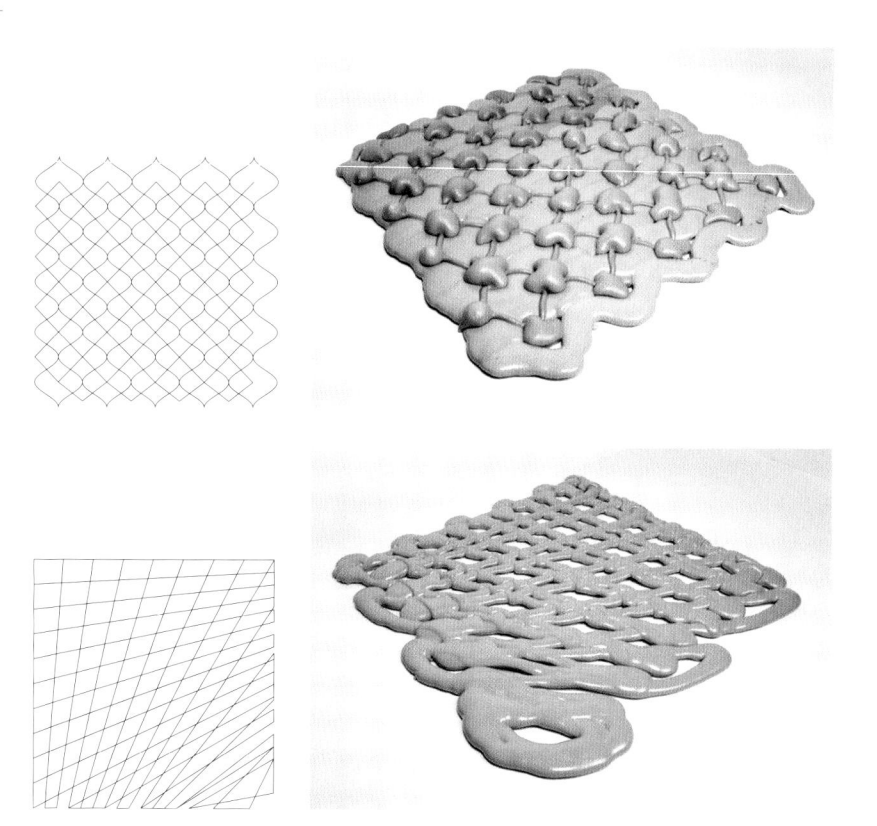

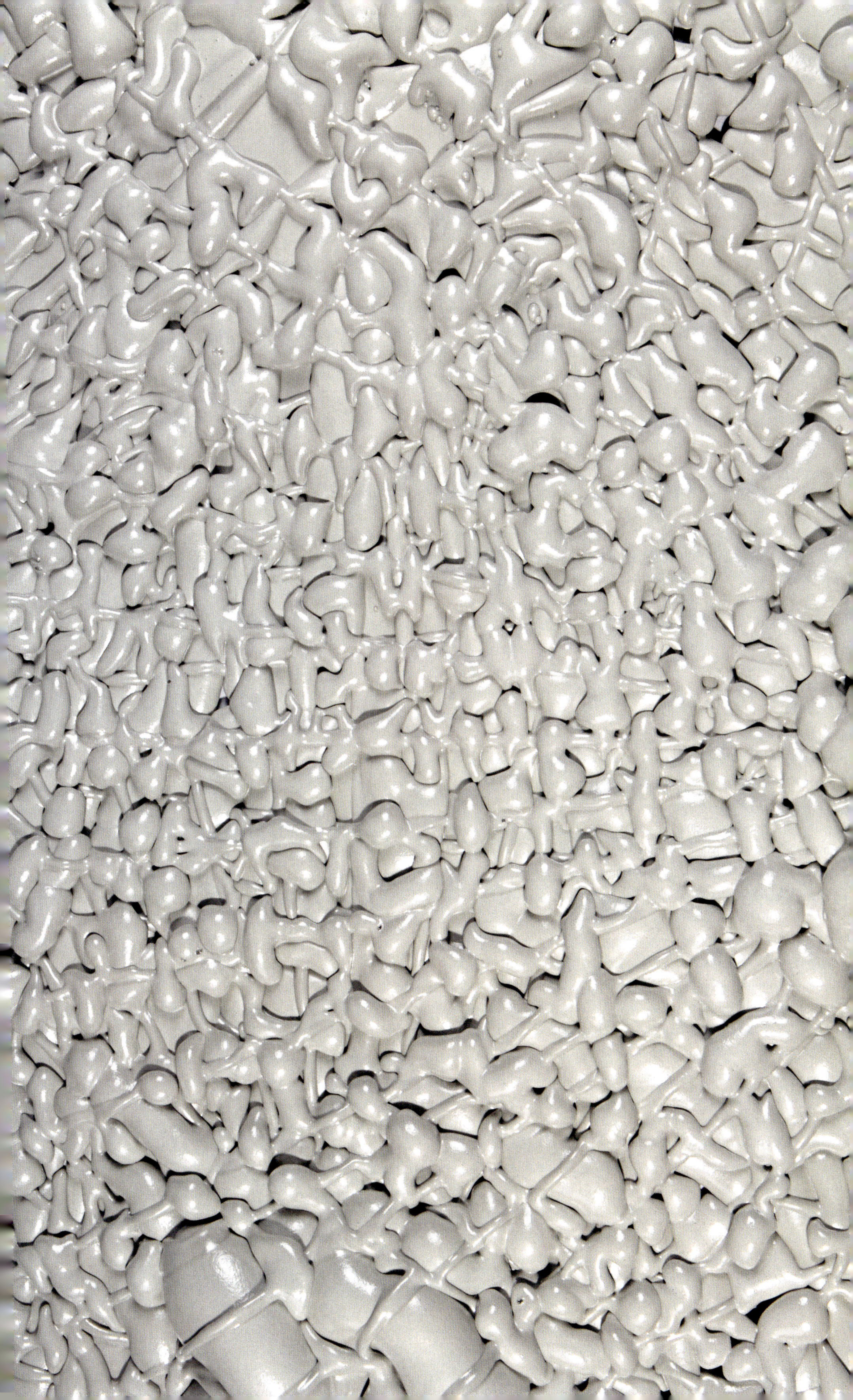

ACOUSTIC DIFFUSORS, 2008. During the second part of the project we investigated adapting the foaming process for the design of active acoustic wall panels. The students engaged with the question of how diffuse reflecting acoustic panels affect the perception of space and the synaesthetic experience between hearing and seeing. Applying algorithmic design tools enabled the parameterised adaptation of the panels to a variety of different spatial and acoustic situations.

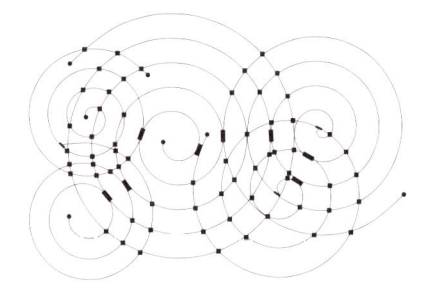

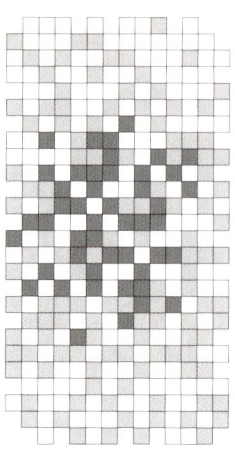

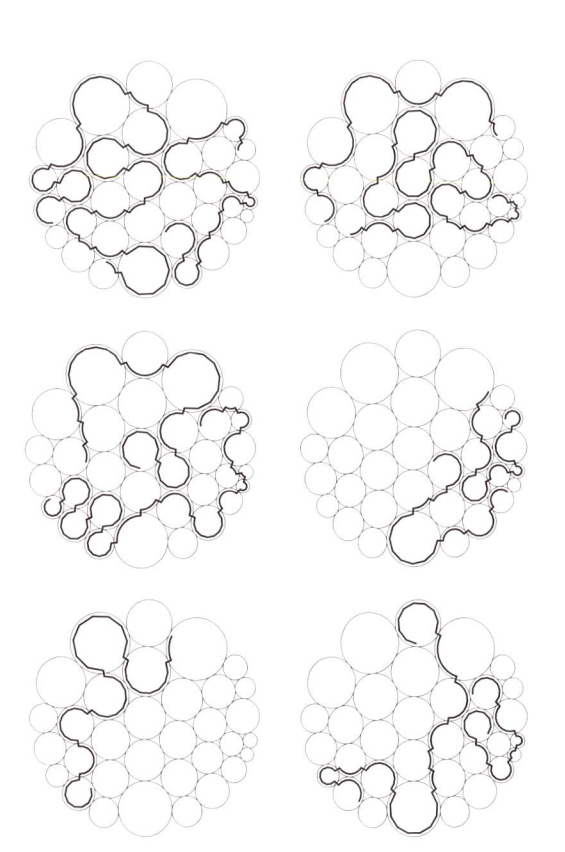

FOAM MONSTER, 2008

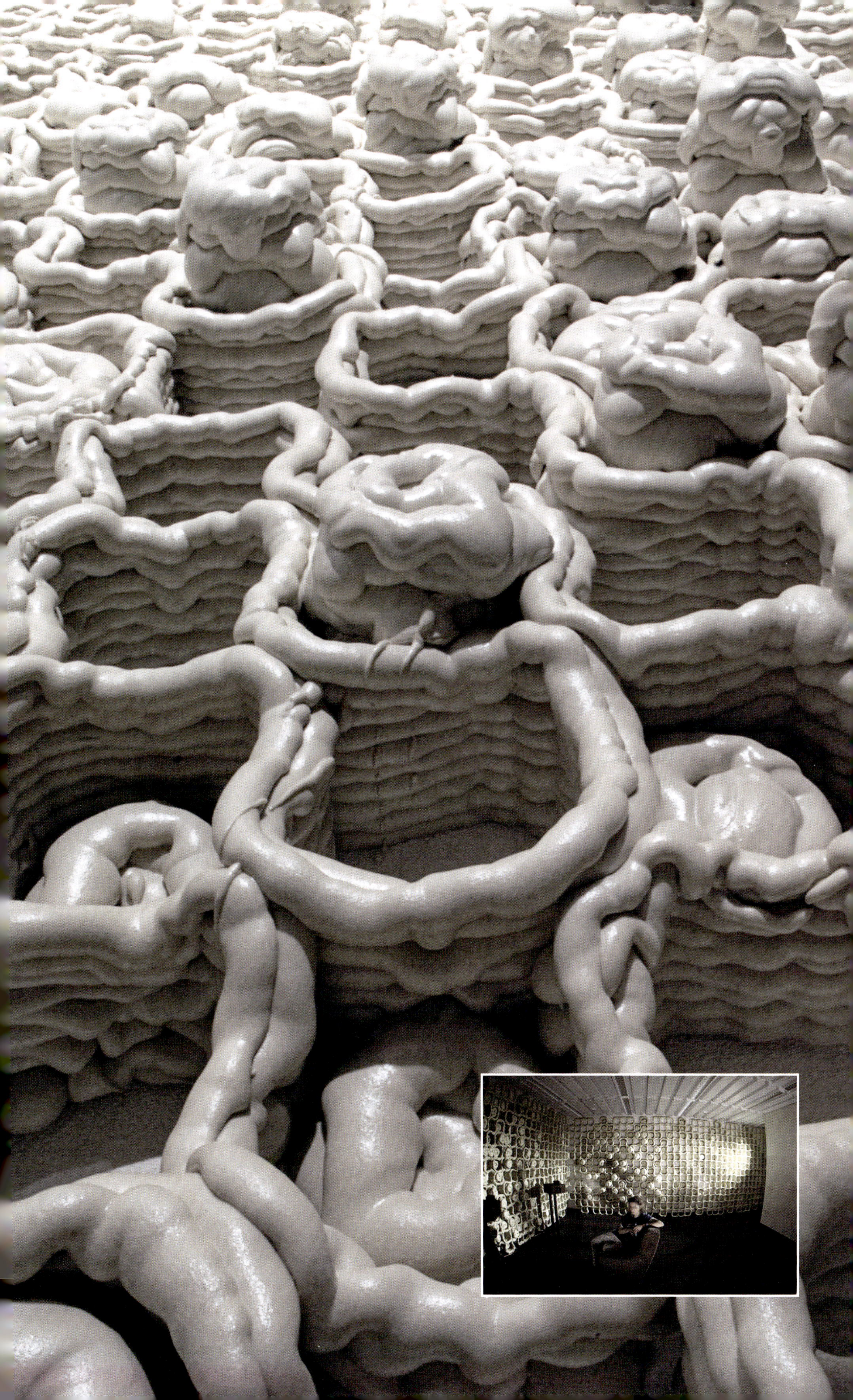

THE SEQUENTIAL WALL, 2008. This project investigates the architectonic and constructive potential of additive digital fabrication in timber construction. We designed a process in which the robot first cut commercially available wooden slats to length and then stacked them in a free arrangement. Such free arrangements allow high-resolution and subtle movements and transitions to be designed, running counter to the modular expression of the stacking. Straight lines flow seamlessly into curved ones, and on the wall's surface an interplay is produced between the rhythmic repetition of the directional wooden slats and the fine gradation of their lengths.

Specially developed algorithmic tools allowed the students to integrate the functional requirements of an external timber wall—for example its loadbearing and insulating behavior as well as its constructive waterproofing—into their designs systems as generative parameters. Functional and formal characteristics were so tightly intertwined that they became mutually dependent. Individual wooden slats that protruded outwards and face down, for example, were used not just as a strongly expressive design element, but also to shield the structural parts from water by channeling it away from the façade, much as pine needles or shingles do.

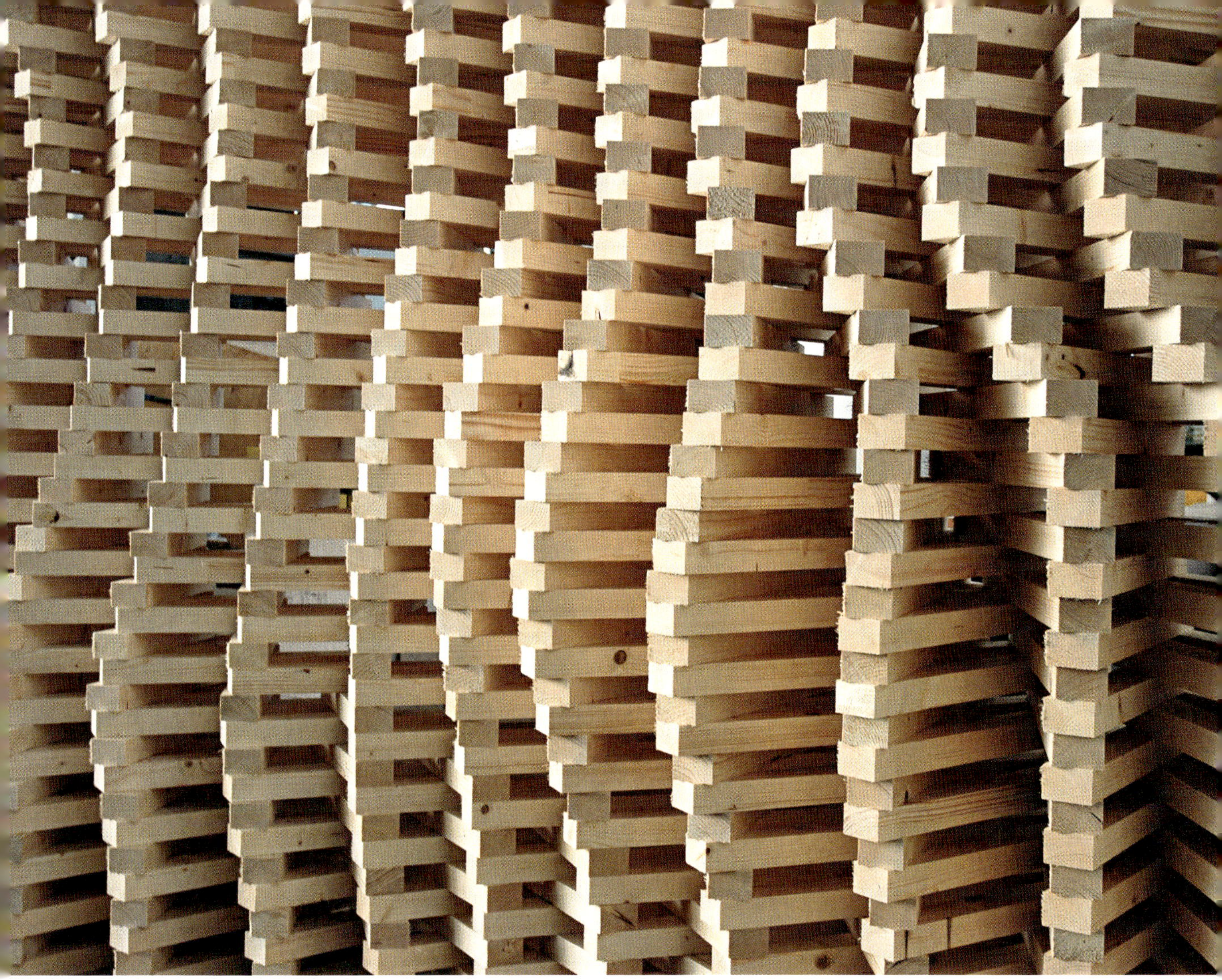

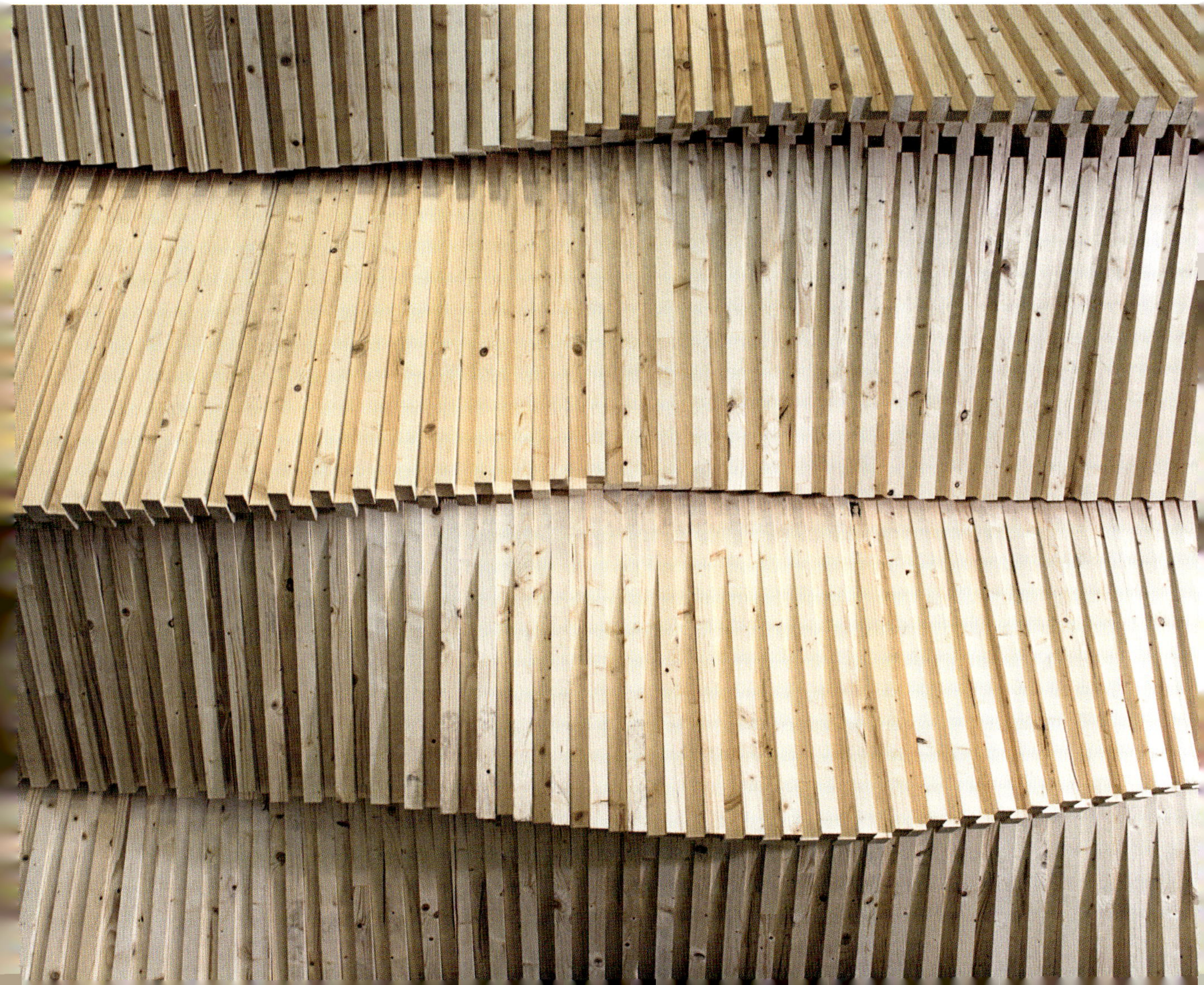

72

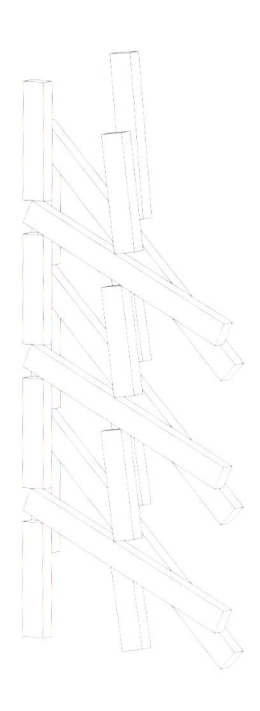

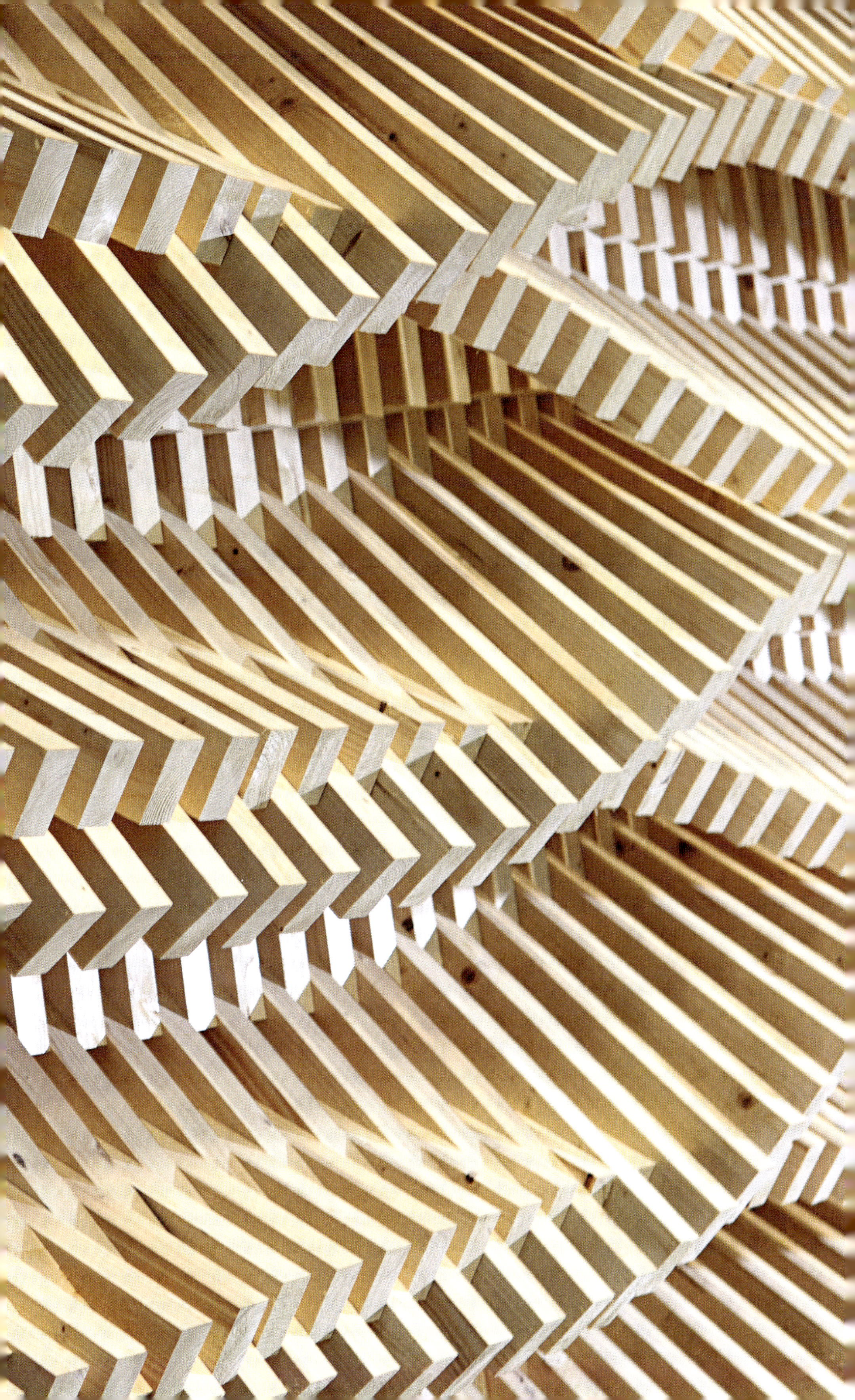

Interjections III

Your focus on software development to digitally design and fabricate building components results in objects of remarkable ontological status. On one hand, their origin in mathematical algorithms such as the Voronoi diagrams surrounds them with an air of objectivity. On the other hand, the appearance of the brick or concrete panels, determined by mathematical calculation and fabricated by industrial robots, bears a close resemblance to the ornamental craftsmanship of the 19th century. Indeed, even the woven character of the patterns can be explained using Gottfried Semper's theory of architecture. How would you characterize your relationship to this "ornamentalism"? Don't you think that the decorative effect of the object would require the discussion of issues of aesthetic perception, rather than focusing exclusively on the technology of fabrication?
ÁKOS MORAVÁNSKY

What is the role of making in architectural design?
What should architects make?
What are the "things" Gramazio & Kohler either couldn't or wouldn't make and why?
Is digital fabrication necessary today in architectural design?
If yes, why?
How would you describe an "architectural robot"?
What would such a device do?
BRANKO KOLAREVIĆ

Materiality does not really begin with matter. The possibility of producing material undercuts, recesses, self-intersections, holes and other telltale signs of formal complexity is linked to a mathematical model's ability to describe variation, and critically, to our own willingness to qualify it conceptually. Consider for instance the impressive medium of rapid prototyping (RP): unlike the laser-cutter, a technically inferior counterpart to which it may be favorably compared, the one-to-one correspondence RP draws between data model and physical artifact eliminates all need for tectonic interpretation. Is that good or bad? Building without tectonics is a dull proposition, so we are certainly entitled to ask: is rapid prototyping primitive? Is laser cutting advanced? Both systems do one thing very well. I love splitting hairs about instruments because deep down, and even on the surface, their limitations reflect our own.
GEORGE L. LEGENDRE

Gramazio & Kohler's projects and their associated technologies are promising in terms of fresh design approaches. At the same time however, they challenge the protocol of current planning practice. In the analogue age, documents produced by architects and engineers served as the basis for contractors' detailed shop drawings. Modeling software, scripting procedures and computer-aided manufacturing devices enable short-cuts in this process. For example, the code commanding a robot that builds brick walls is written by the architect, or the digital model of a steel structure delivered by the engineer already provides enough information to laser cut actual material in the workshop. This advance in technology comes along with blurring the borders of accountability. Our question therefore is how this affects the distribution of responsibilities. Who is liable for precision, quality, costs, time schedules or even incorrect components on the job site?

Digitalization of planning and building needs an appropriate legal framework that controls the relationship of planners and contractors and their contribution to the common work under changing technological realities. While there is a smooth digital workflow in the automobile and airplane industry, the building sector seems to lack reliable codes that would be necessary to speed up digital planning. Can generative practice help in gaining experience that is able to challenge and redefine the rigid framework of these burdensome codes? What would be the vision towards future developments?
MANFRED GROHMANN, OLIVER TESSMANN

From an historic deterministic perspective, architecture can be viewed as a technological system that is expressed by supposedly "objective" parameters such as production process or material. Accordingly, the history of architecture can be understood to be a history of its technological development measured in innovations in construction or functional refinements. But architecture belongs also to the field of objects. Therefore, technological change leads not only to changes in the built environment, but also in how we use and perceive it. Consequently, the impact of these changes on our experience of the environment is decisive, even beyond the mechanization or digitalization of architecture. Therefore form is ultimately at the forefront of any design work and is more significant than mastering the technological means. LAURENT STALDER

How does applying diverse software environments from the design phase through to the production phase effect the relationship between intentional and "accidental" design? Can the never-ending "loop" of calculated changes to design parameters and, conversely, making a selection from an infinite number of permutations be defined as a method? Which strategies do you apply, or do you think are possible to apply, to productively link these aspects of designing with the architect's perspective, as protagonist and viewer, which it ultimately involves?

For example, could an "exit" option be formulated, as in computer programs, which brings the loop to an end, etc.? TIM ELDER

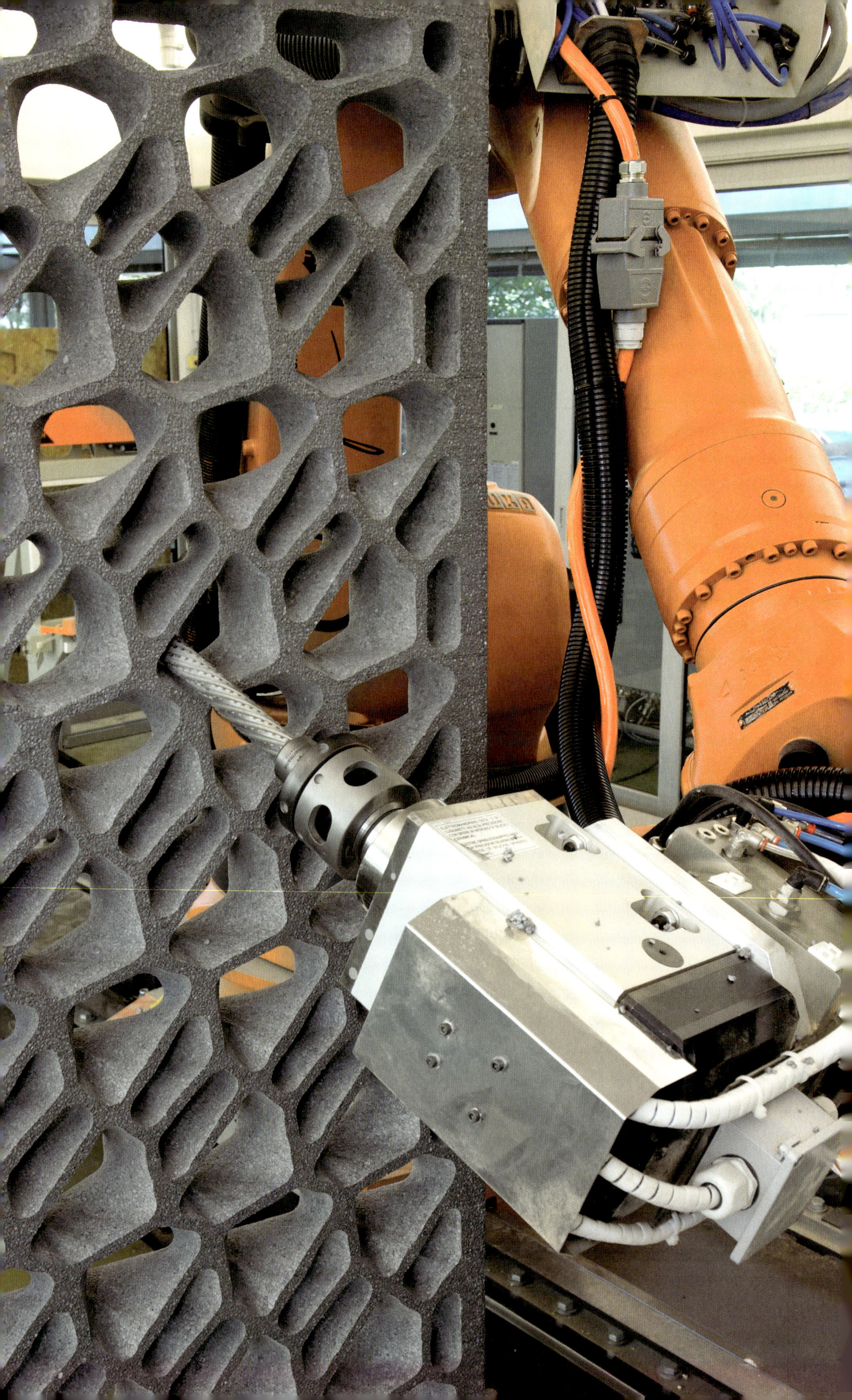

TAKING AWAY
RESEARCH AND TEACHING PROJECTS ON PERFORATIONS, ETH ZURICH

What is a hole? A hole is an open, hollow space. It is created by the removal of material, and its form and character are determined by the material remaining around it. In architecture, holes are openings that link internal and external spaces, and open views into and out of them. Properties such as dimension, position, angle, depth of reveals, and contour determine their spatial effect and architectonic expression. Several closely adjacent holes are perceived as perforations and, according to the density and form of the individual holes, the observer's attention is drawn either to them or to the structure of the surrounding material. Perforated structures are employed in architecture to fulfill contradictory requirements: functionally they separate spaces from one another, and yet their transparency acts to communicate and connect. By disclosing the depth of their construction, such walls unfurl a distinct presence and offer diverse potential for spatial design.

Using digital fabrication methods that do not depend on repetition or a uniform grid, highly differentiated perforated wall elements can be produced. Since it is possible to shape the forms of the cut-outs and reveals of the individual openings, the front and reverse sides of the wall can take on different characters. And depending on the angle at which the holes penetrate the wall, the perspective is steered in a particular direction. Through the differing orientations of several openings, permeable areas are created in the wall, their form and transparency changing continuously and gently along with the movement of the observer. The wall thus gains in visual presence and depth effect.

But how can large numbers of varied architectonic openings be designed? The technical feasibility of such complex and differentiated structures using digital fabrication requires the architect to develop and master concepts, methods and tools for controlling the continuous variation of such quantities of information. In addition to exploring constructive strategies, therefore, the definition of design logics forms a fundamental element of our investigations.

THE OBLIQUE HOLE, 2005–2006. We confronted the students with the task of distributing 2000 slanted holes over an irregular polygonal volume. Since this quantity of information cannot be managed with conventional CAD, we developed our own algorithmic tools. The density distribution was achieved through modeling an information landscape that completely enveloped the volume. A large distance between this body and this surface generated a high density of holes, and a smaller distance a low density. A further tool enabled the students to orient the holes towards positions that could be placed freely in space. They could also grasp topological characteristics of the holes, such as their position in relation to the edges or corners of the body, and use this information again for their own logic of distribution and orientation.

Despite reducing the medium of design to the single boring of a hole, surprising architectonic artifact were created. The polygonal volumes were designed continuously beyond their corners, various surfaces coalesced, sharp room edges softened, and new, visual surfaces were created that overlapped the volume's geometry. When entire fields of holes were oriented towards one point in space, the view from exactly this point turned the plastic depth of the material into an abstract—almost depthless—surface.

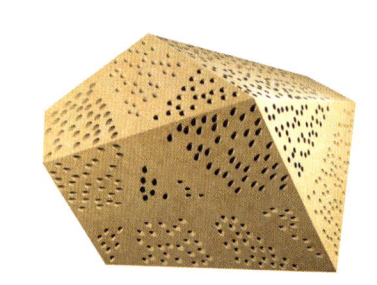

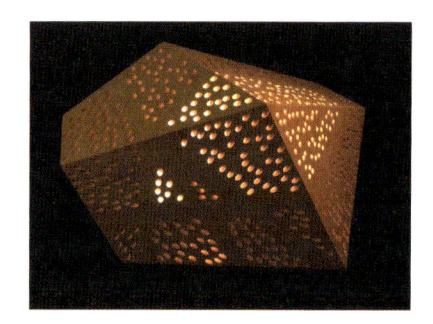

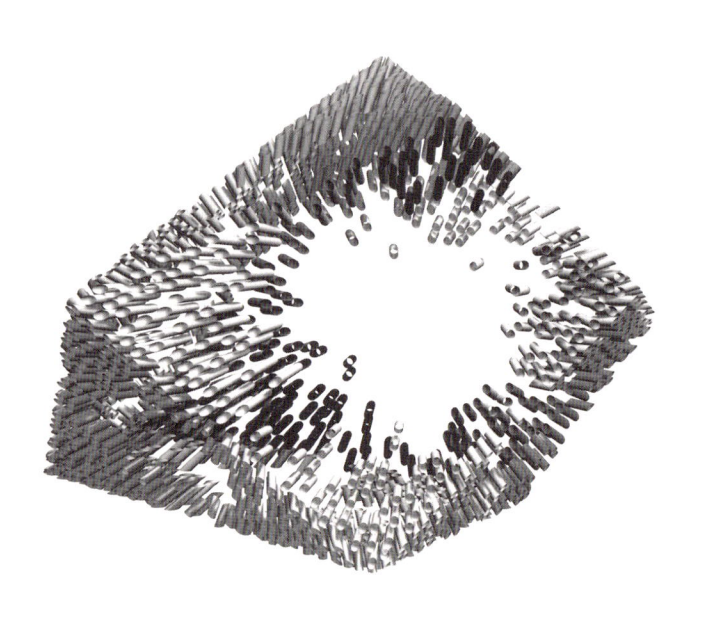

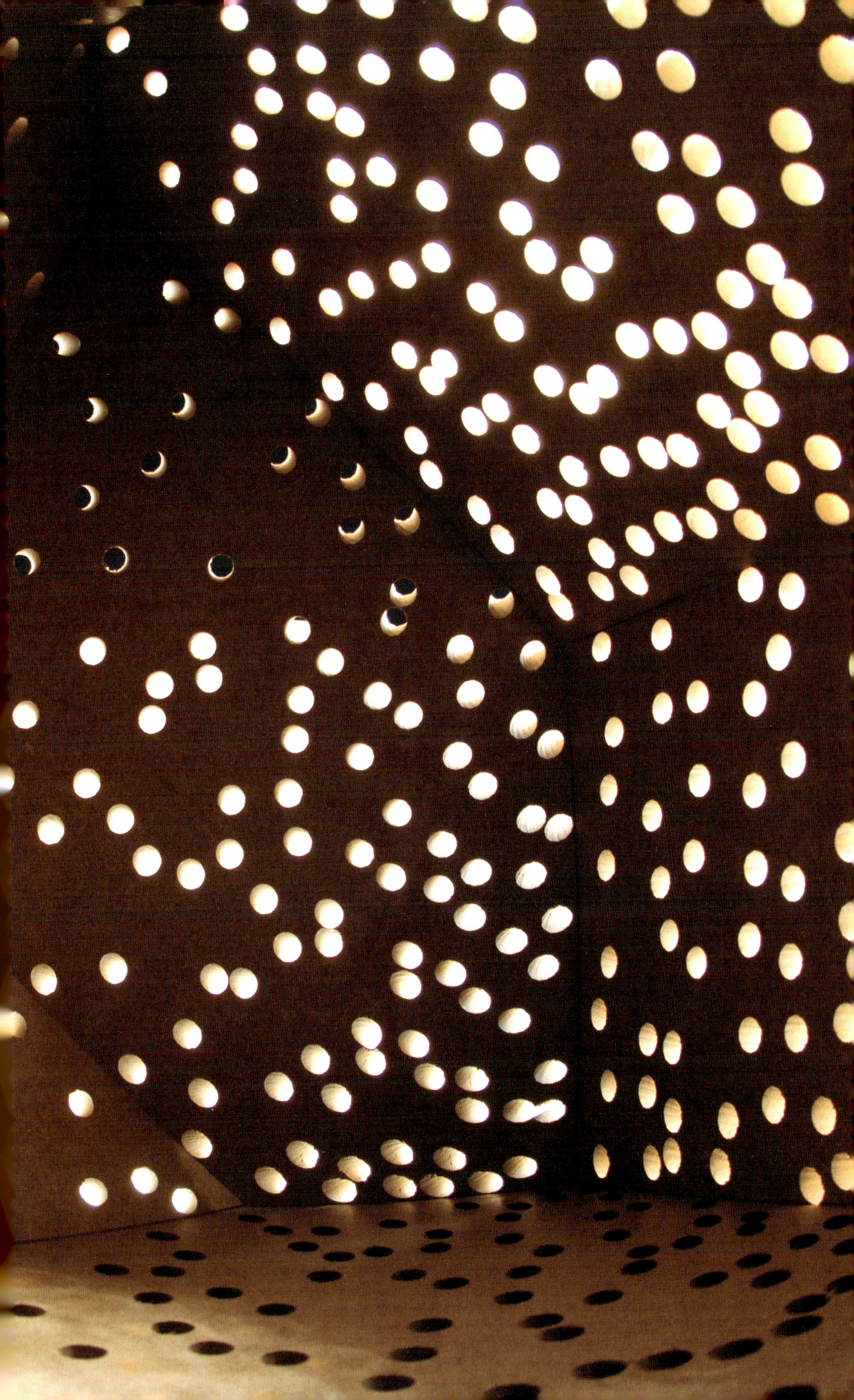

THE PERFORATED WALL, 2006. The architectural potential of perforations was investigated in a 1:1 building element. After several design studies and the manufacture of prototypes from polystyrene panels, two walls were realized in concrete.

The individual holes could be controlled in terms of four parameters: their position, the angle of their deflection from the surface, their rotation about their center, and their size. Their distribution on the wall could be designed through globally acting forces of attraction and repulsion; a dynamic system oriented the holes against one another until a state was reached in which there was no overlap. The deflection from the surface and the size of the holes, on the other hand, were controlled via the color values of a digital image file. These algorithmic tools offered the students an intuitive route into design, and were used to complement the programming of their own logics of distribution and orientation.

The production of the perforated concrete walls presented us with a particular technical challenge. Since the irregular arrangement of the holes and the minimal web thicknesses meant that neither classical reinforcement nor mechanical post-compaction of the concrete were possible, a self-compacting steel fiber concrete developed by the Institute for Building Materials at the ETH Zurich was used. Strength tests on various samples showed that highly perforated concrete walls could be used in construction, and that their loadbearing capacity could be directly controlled via the number, density and rotation of the holes. These findings show that perforated walls like these are not just a design variant of traditional room-dividing systems, but that they are also suitable for realizing loadbearing structures.

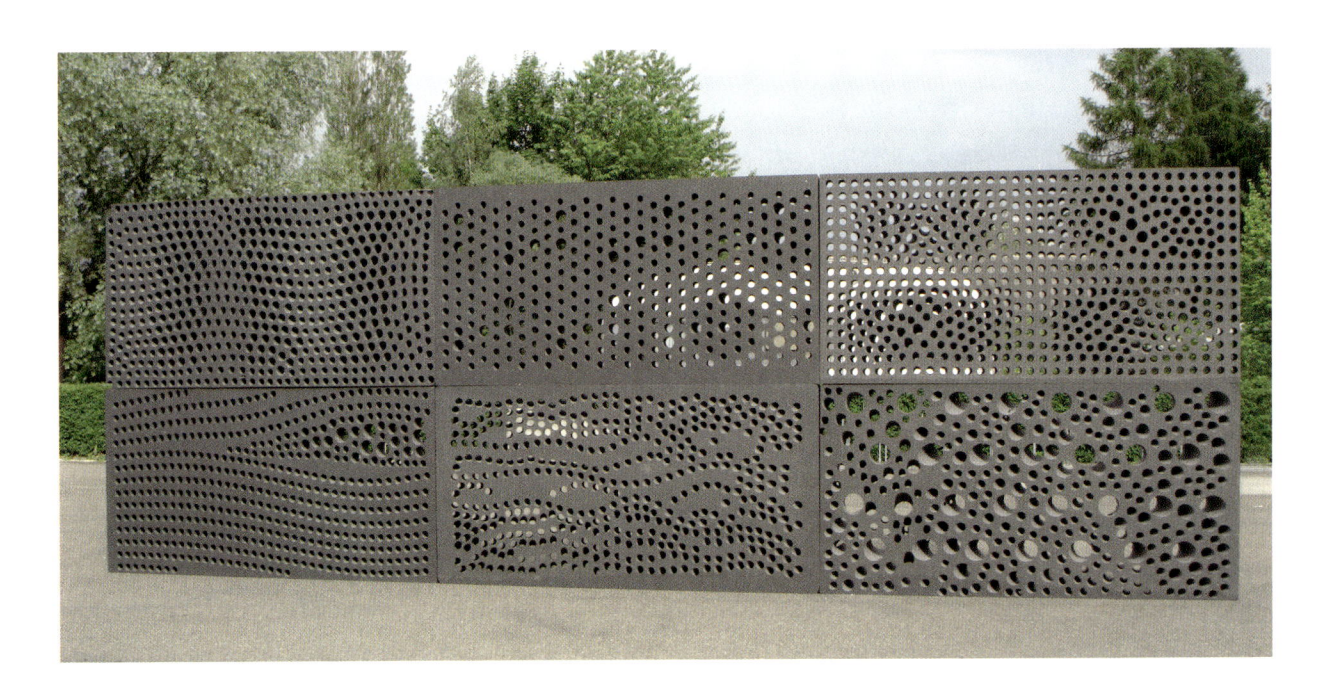

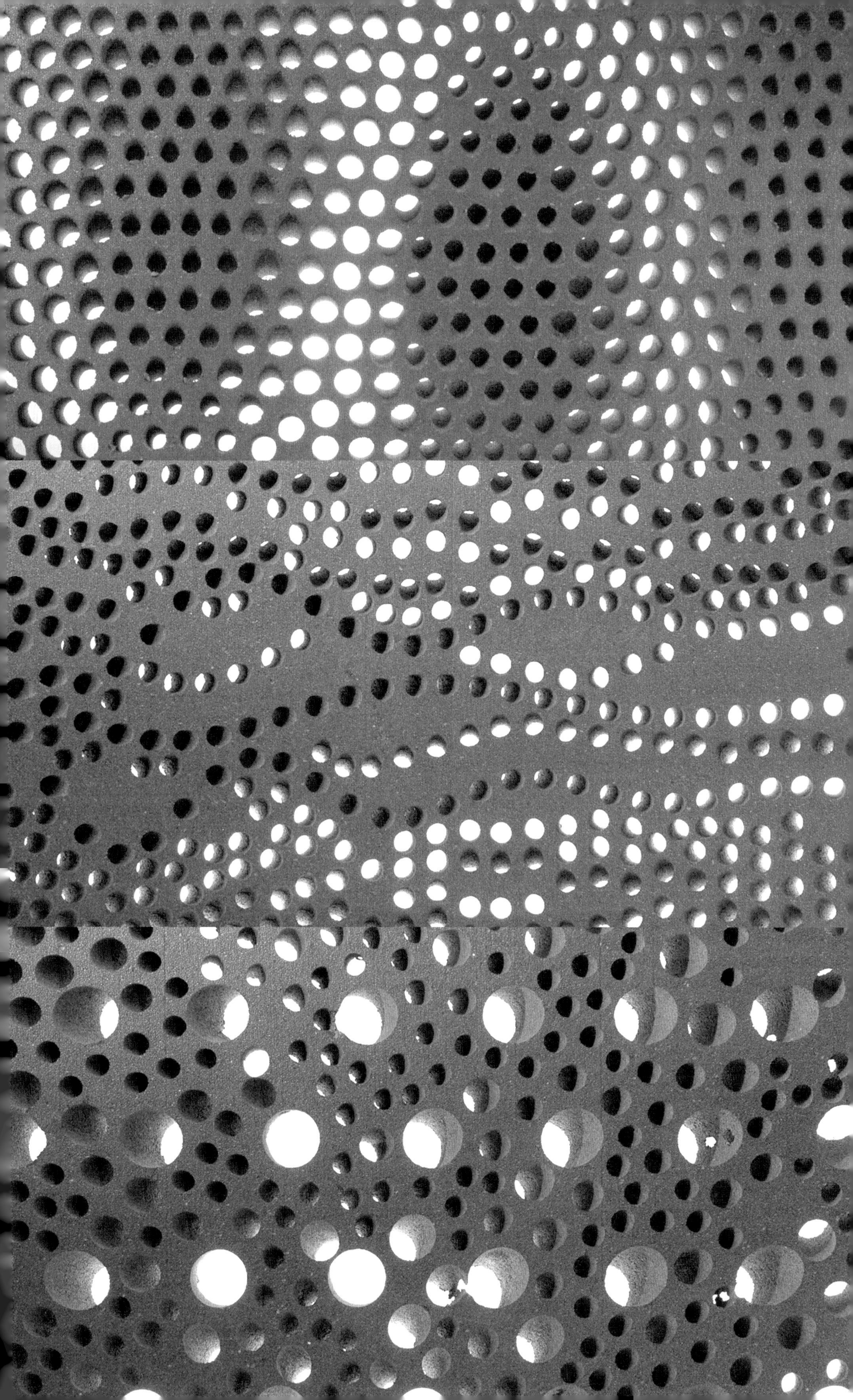

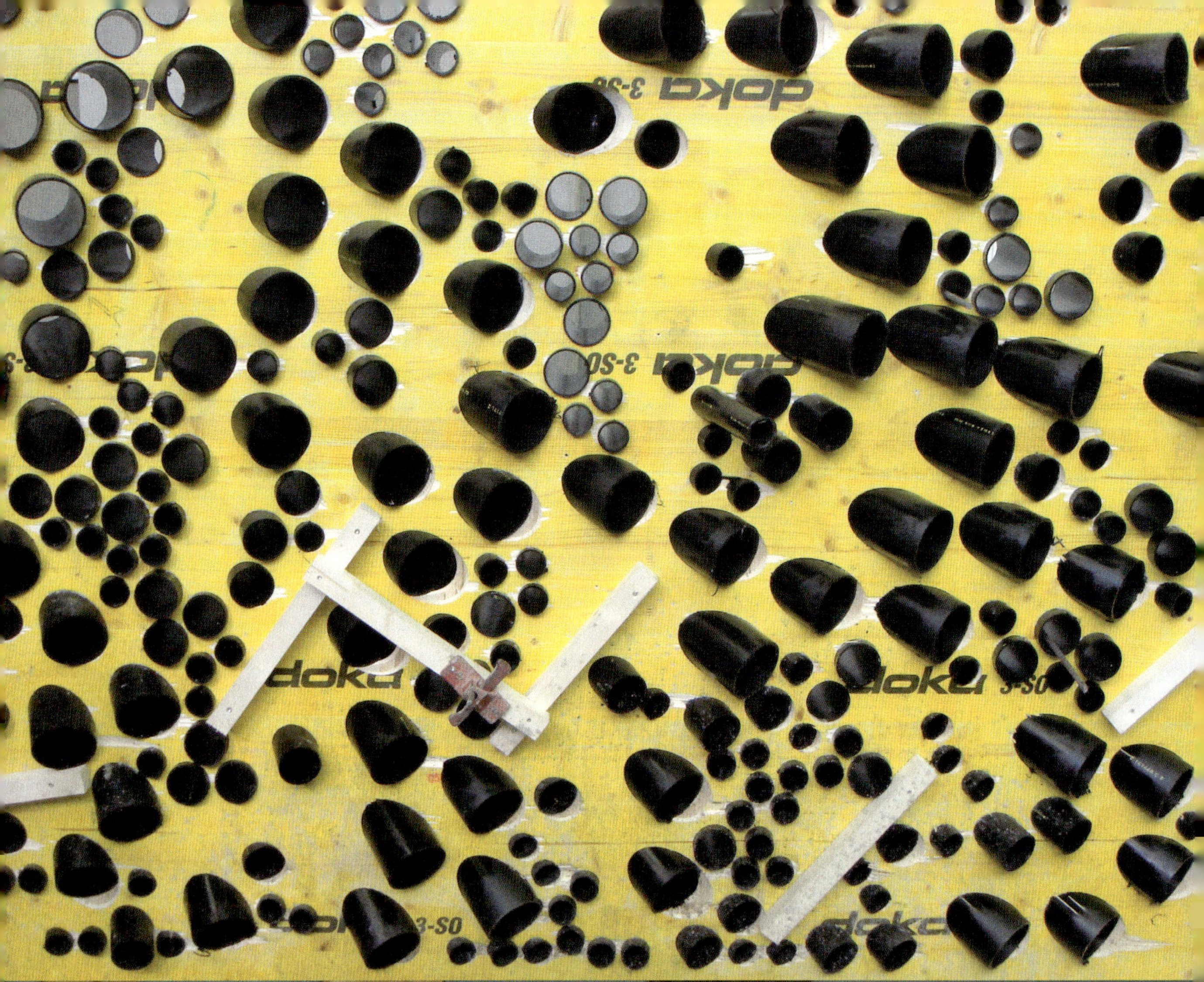
doka 3-SO

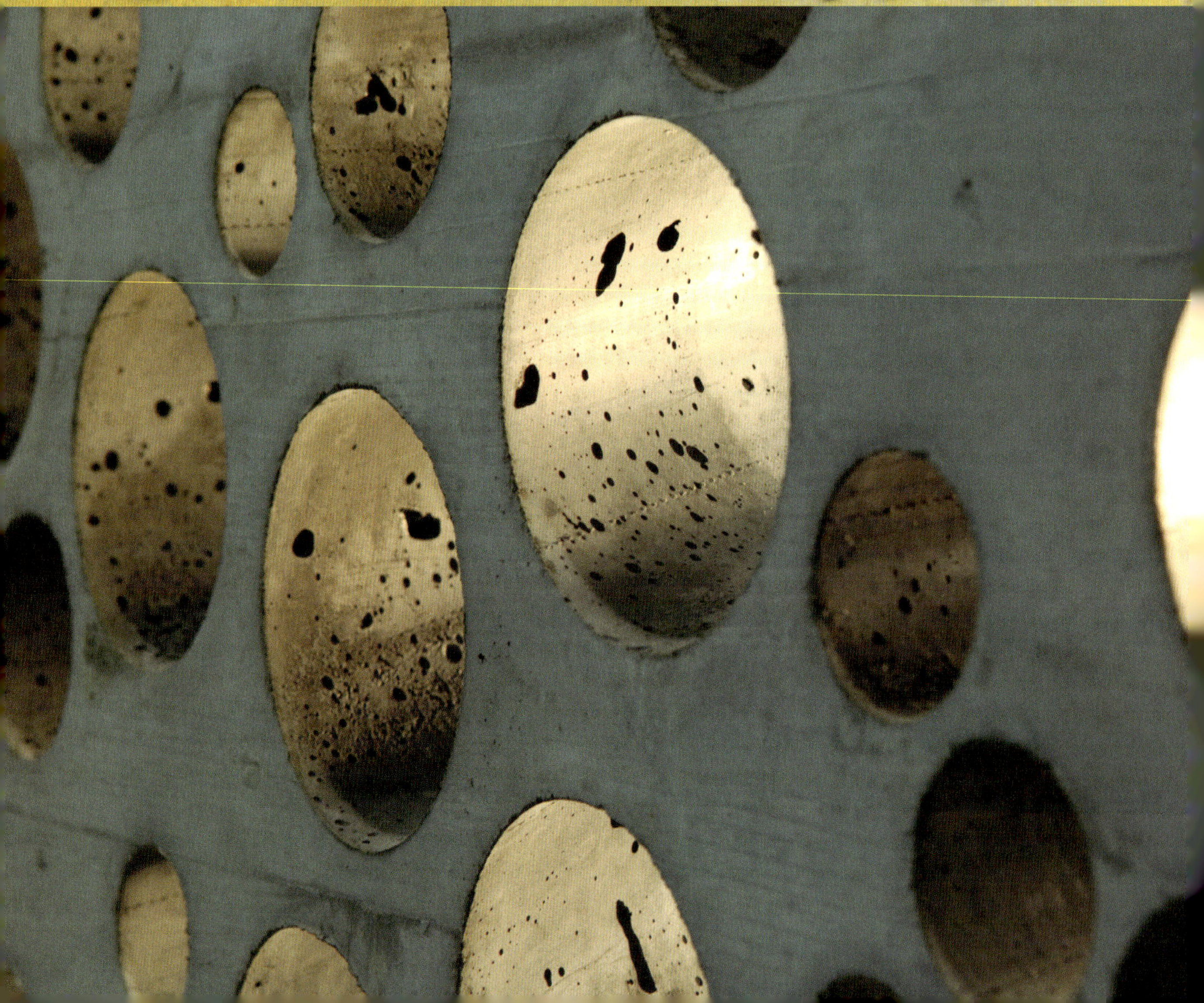

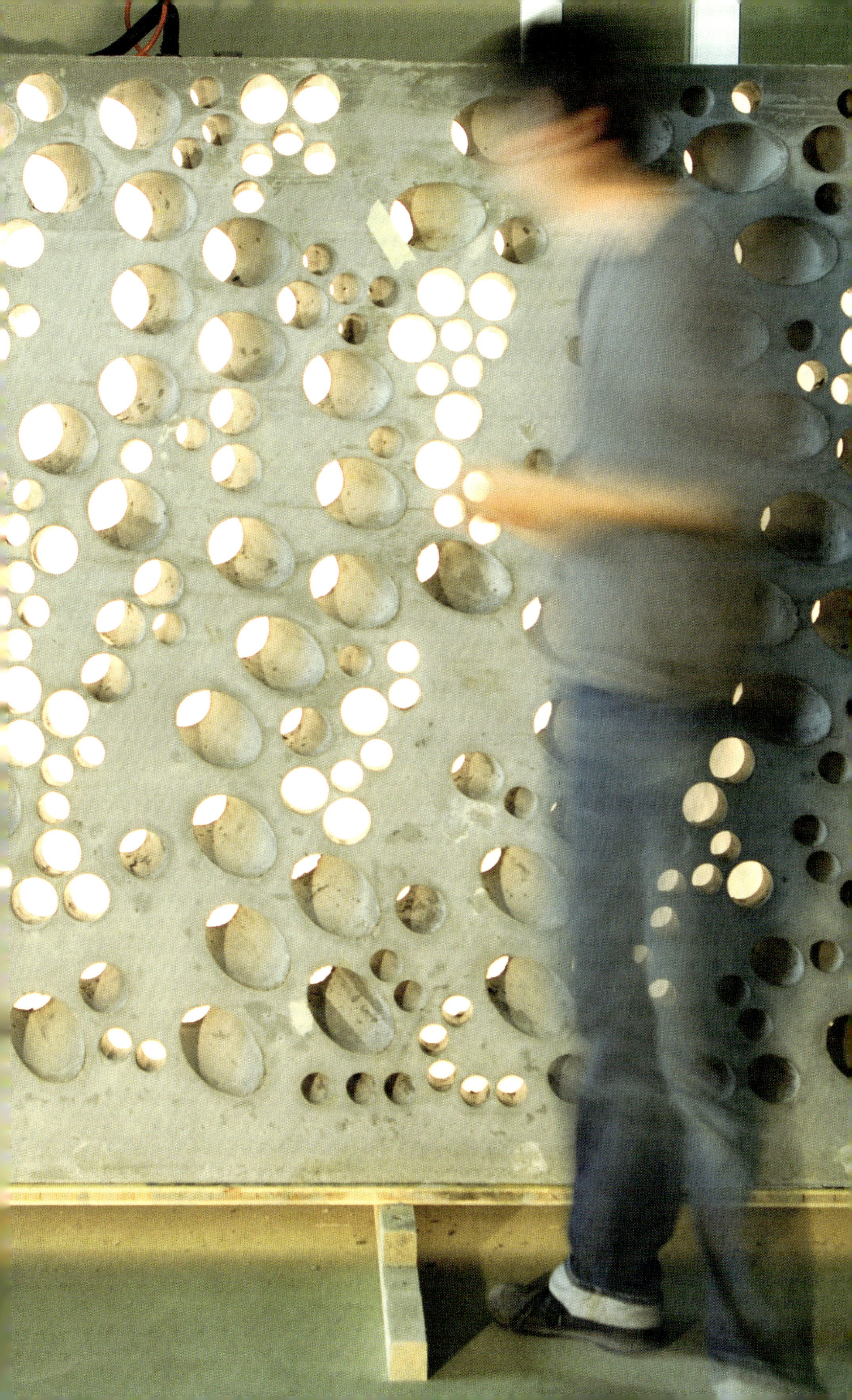

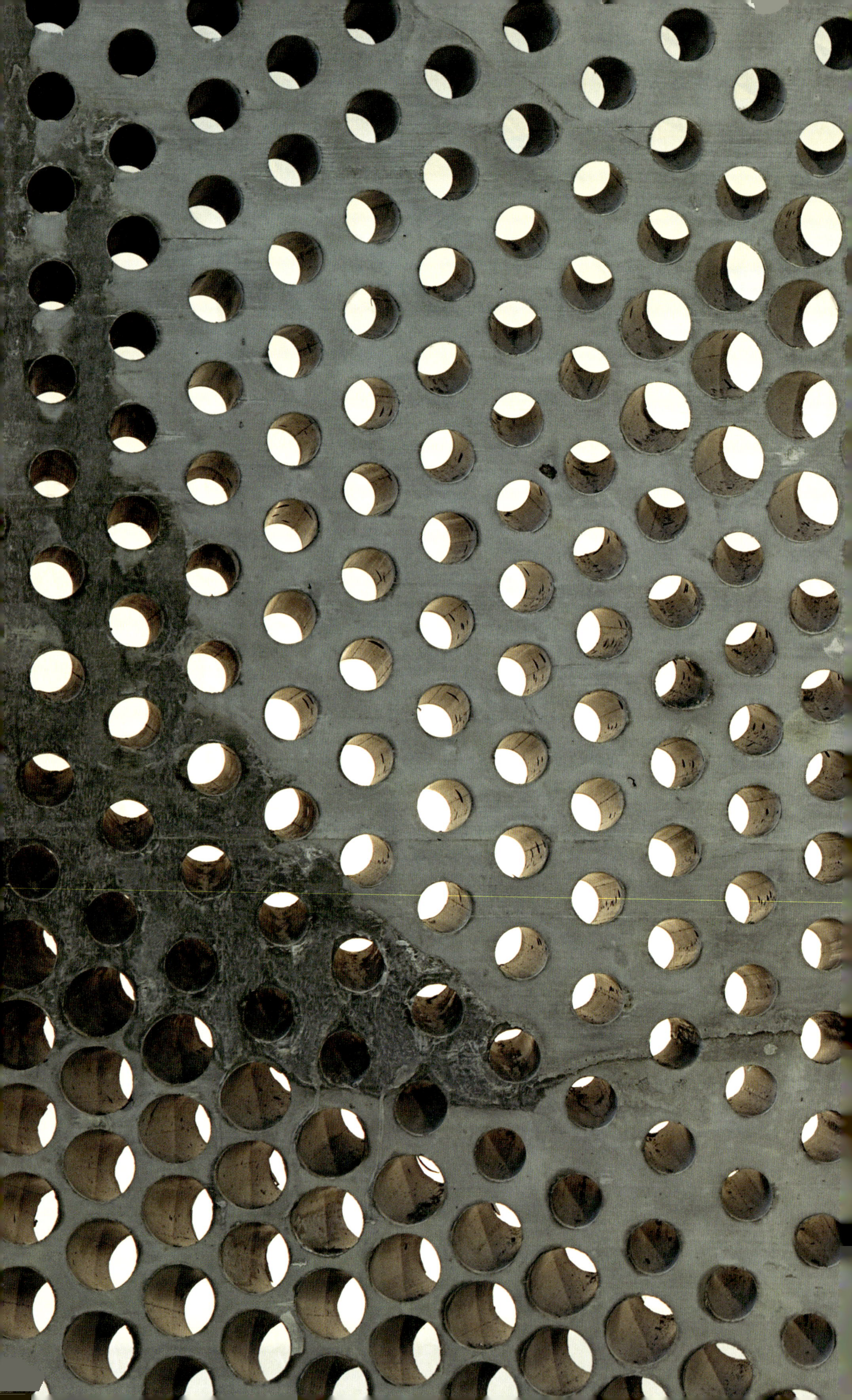

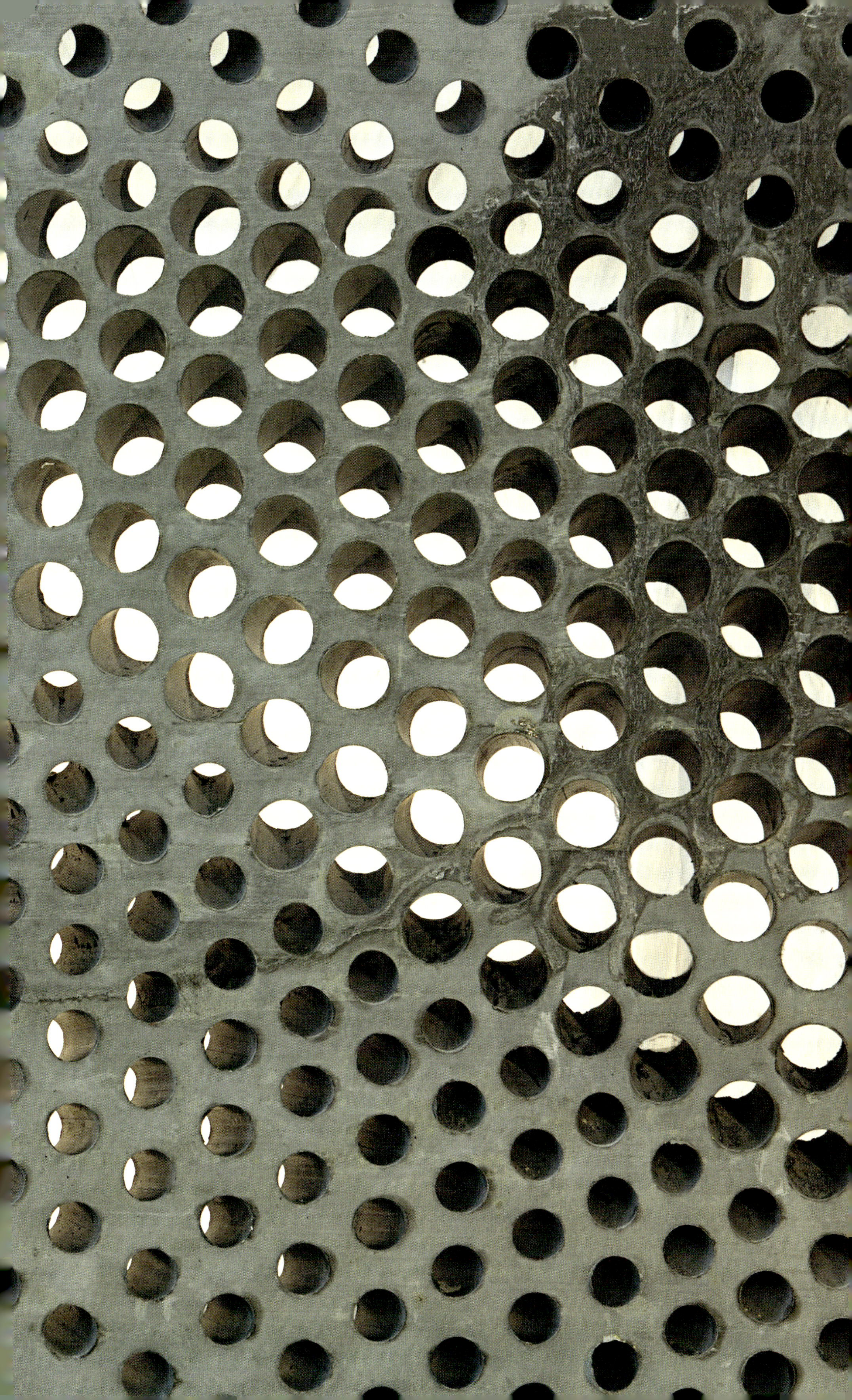

THE DISSOLVED WALL, 2006–2007. In this investigation of screen structures, we extended the vocabulary of aperture forms. These could now take on any desired form, including irregular ones, and have plastically deformed reveals. Using algorithmic tools the students placed points on the wall's surface. From this field of points, the mathematical method of the Voronoi diagram was then used to derive a polygonal division of the surfaces which, mapped on both sides and connected to each other, produced a two-and-a-half-dimensional grid structure. By shifting the points on the front and back of the wall, one could plastically deform the reveals of the apertures and thus shape the screen structure.

Another unusual design medium was derived from the fabrication process. The robot normally mills along the shortest connection between the two contours of the aperture. If one shifts these connection points, the aperture tapers towards the center of the cross section. One fascinating aspect of this technique, which we call "Spin," is that the simple combination of the tool's form and path produces complex and extremely expressive plastic deformations of the apertures' reveals, without these complex surfaces having to be described geometrically. The screen structures produced in this way are sharply distinguished from each other in their formal expression—this ranges from geometric progressions through spatial ornaments to apparently organically grown structures—yet all have an astonishing effect of depth and plasticity.

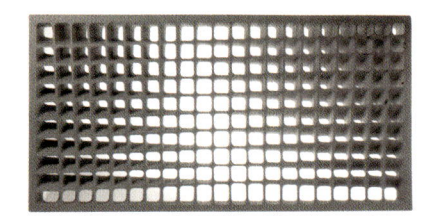

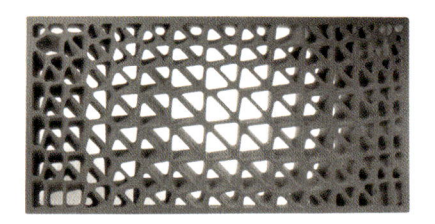

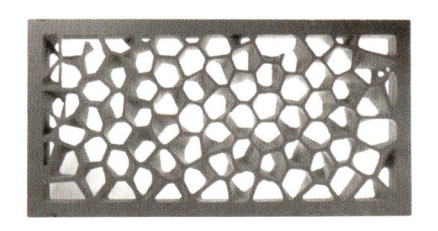

SCIENCE CITY CONSTRUCTION HOARDING, ZURICH, 2007–2012. The design potential of the screen structures was tested on a hoarding system for building sites on the ETH Zurich campus. Perforations were used specifically to give views of what was happening inside the fence, while ensuring the necessary security for the building site. Although the designs focused on the large-scale presence of these temporary interventions, the students also had to pay attention to the close-up effects generated.

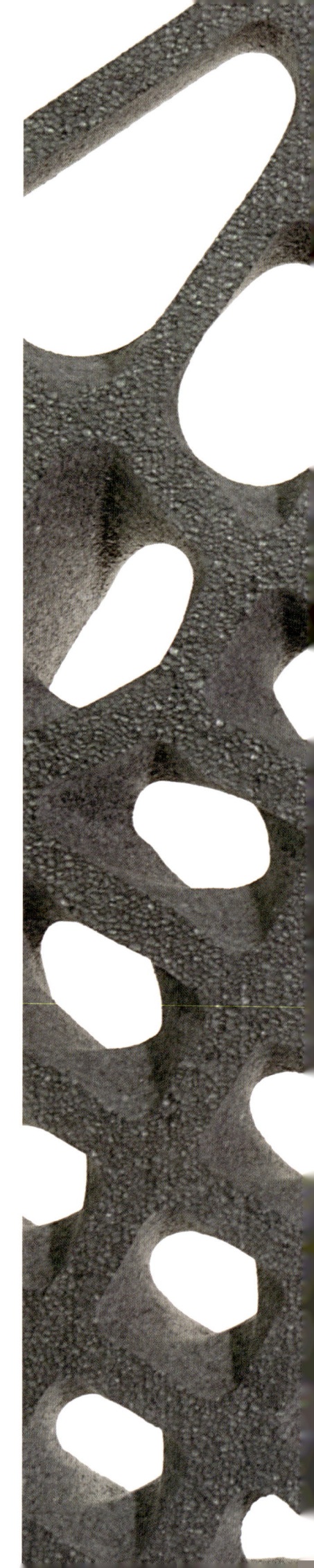

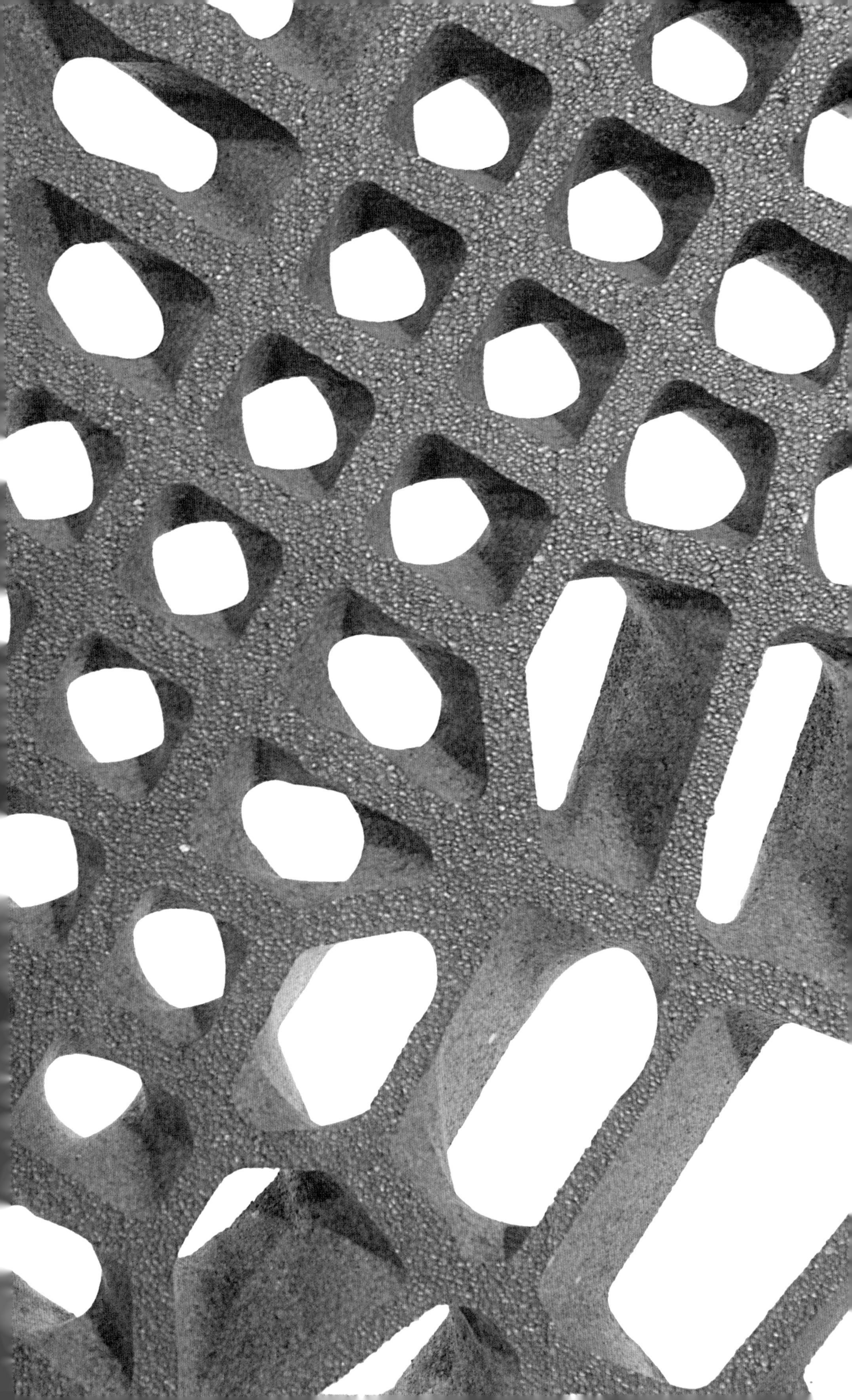

RUBIK

SCIENCE CITY HOUSING, ZURICH, COMPETITION 2008

Each of the five student apartment towers is unique—just like its 441 possible inhabitants. None of the flats and none of the rooms is identical to another. The varied positions and proportions of the windows thus underscore the individual geometry of the rooms, while ensuring equivalent apertures for each room. The closed surface of the façade emphasizes this variation with a motive of closely adjacent circles. The ground plans of the flats obey the principle of greatest possible variation, at the same time providing maximum sightlines between the lounges of the individual living units. Algorithms controlled the design so that the desired diversity could be achieved.

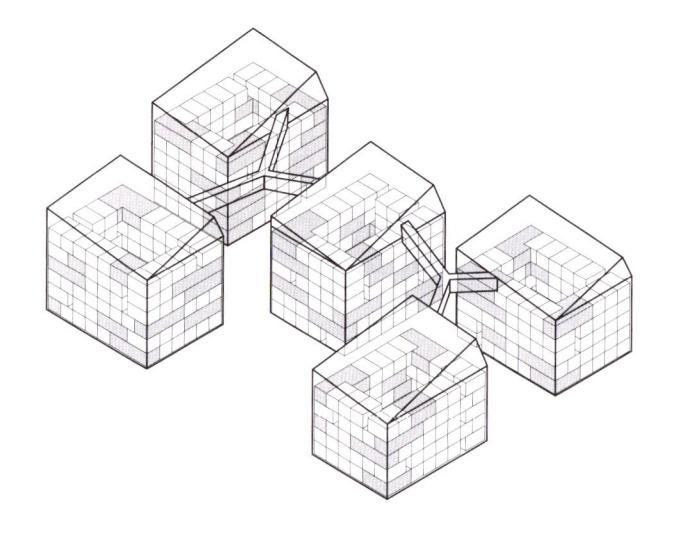

89

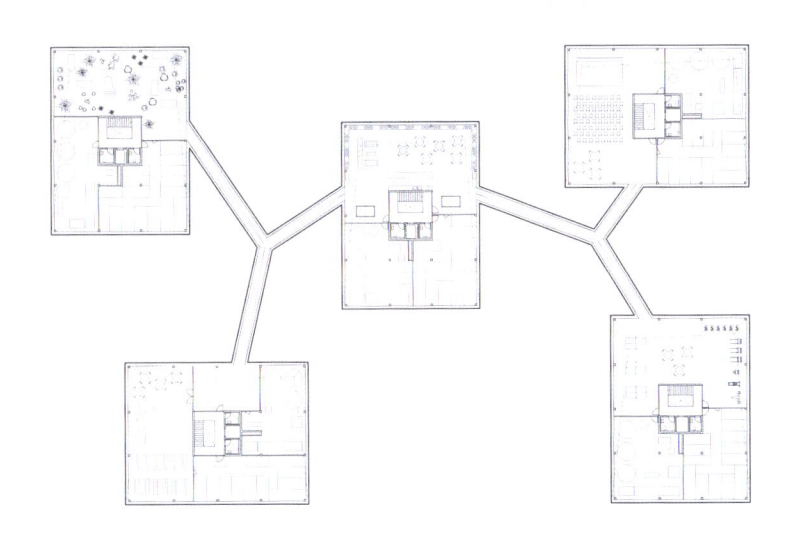

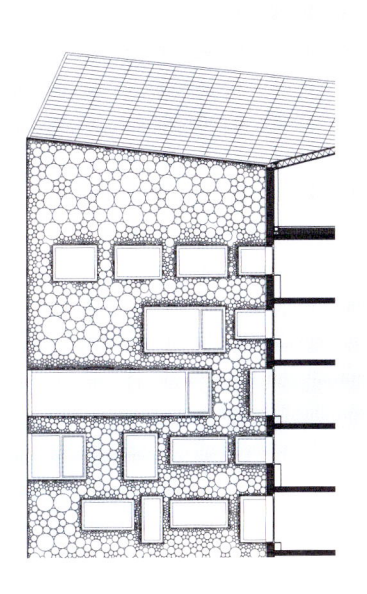

Interjections IV

The forms now made possible by digital design tools and computer-integrated manufacturing are highly expressive. It seems easier to craft them technically than to master them architecturally. It even seems that technical feasibility has outdone the visions of those engaged in form finding. What do you think is needed aesthetically and perhaps ethically for engendering the capability to motivate architecturally the expressionism that is rendered feasible by way of technology?
GEORG FRANCK

THE SECOND LIFE OF ICARUS
If it didn't have such a tragic end, the myth of Icarus would be a perfect metaphor for Gramazio & Kohler's work. What if Icarus would have survived his fall? He might have discovered that his wings could actually help him swim and would have been quite content in the water. Similarly, Gramazio & Kohler represent a certain downfall of utopia, a plunge into concrete reality after years of abstract dreaming: from sky to water, void to solid, from the absence of resistance in the air to the viscous density of water, from the 1990s to the 2000s. It's like the fall of the numeric technologies first explored by people like Greg Lynn, Marcos Novak or fabric.ch in the 1990s: today these technologies are confronted with the constraints of building materials and the messy, cumbersome construction methods of the real world. But maybe these technologies are quite comfortable there; maybe this confrontation could create a sort of "pragmatic utopia."

I remember reading an article ten years ago in the French newspaper *Libération* on NASA's predictions of what future dwellings on Mars would look like. Surprisingly enough, NASA envisioned semi-troglodyte vaulted caves built out of bricks that would be made from the planet's ferrous dust and baked at 900°C in solar reflecting kilns. Their archaic appearance totally clashed with the slick high-tech visions of the future that were so popular in the 1960s. The Gantenbein Winery is exactly this kind of prosaic confrontation between new technologies and lowly materialism.

Could one say that Swiss architecture has been marked by its own particular downfall of utopia—one without delusion or bitterness? Think of 1940s modernism, where the precepts of early modernism were deviated by the use of traditional materials and simple building techniques, as in the architecture of Hans Leuzinger or Hans Fischli (who is now more known as the father of Peter Fischli from Fischli & Weiss). More recently, the early work of Herzog & de Meuron or Peter Zumthor totally perverted post-modernism by shifting attention from form to materials. My own work is also a sort of material deviation, where a certain physiological, biological or chemical depth is given to the immateriality of contemporary communication media and abstract globalized space. PHILIPPE RAHM

How do CNC technologies influence the design of complex three-dimensional parts that will be set to motion for the sake of kinetic and interactive projects?

In terms of acceptance of interactive architecture which combines kinetics and sensing, the issue of failure is paramount. While there is already precedent such as elevators, escalators, automatic garage doors etc., there is a wealth of new architectural systems which are becoming more prevalent in architecture. For novel systems without precedent, what can CNC fabrication contribute to the challenges that face interactive architectural subsystems from a reliability and dependability standpoint?

The automotive, aerospace and even maritime industries have reached a far more developed state in terms of being both intelligent and mechanical than that of architecture. Architecture is really in its infancy from an application standpoint relative to interaction design. These other industries benefit greatly from mass-production in terms of cost reduction, and the investment afforded to design. Good architecture on the other hand is dependent upon one-off originality, which directly affects the design investment ratio. What are the benefits of CNC technologies in terms of original design cross-referenced with original fabrication costs? MICHAEL FOX

Fabio Gramazio and Matthias Kohler are architects. But what are Gramazio & Kohler?

Some might say that they are choreographers of digital design and fabrication processes, or scenographers of an apparently seamless robotic determinism—today's digital Wizards of Oz. Others would describe them as the facilitators of economically viable assembly methods that allow for variation and intricacy, or the authors of computerized production chains subject to adapted scripts of parametric optimization. They could be regarded as reluctant ornamentalists who favor the recognizable aesthetics and communicative power of figurative representation over the symbolic indeterminacy of the mathematical diagram. Are they the couturiers of the curtain-wall, applying Semper's ornamental principle of the textile partition to contemporary tectonic elements? Looking at its output we may concede their practice to be an artistic one: material qualities, be they morphological or aesthetic, precondition all their projects in pursuit of an architectural expression of amplified sensuality. Are they fetishists favoring texture and tactility over digital incorporeality, while attaining one through the other? Could they be imagineers of visual stimulants or builders of sculptural objectivity, or both simultaneously? Are they breaking out of the puritan Swiss box or are they breaking into its anemic modernist core to reconfigure and reanimate it? What if they are inventors? Not of products or technologies, but of a new role for the architect. What if they are about to save the profession from obsolescence by claiming a central logistical role within contemporary construction processes that engages meaningfully with its various agencies? Their practice revolves around the configuration of material and digital systems, but at its center lies a systematic reconfiguration of architectural practice itself.

So the question remains: what are Gramazio & Kohler? They might be architects, but not as we know them—yet. OLIVER DOMEISEN

How can the digital design/fabrication process reduce the carbon footprint of our societies? How can these fantastic tools/processes be utilized to enable the creation of healthy places for the 80% of the world's population who have nothing? CHRIS LUEBKEMAN

Based on the additive principle of the most archaic individual building unit, Gramazio & Kohler have succeeded in bridging a hegemonic, virtual-hypothetical digital realm with a complex, physical built reality. One must look beyond the mere ornamental beauty of these objects to see the sophisticated exchange between binary codes, industrial robotics, and bricks and mortar. They have exceeded the limitations of typical brick construction to create a novel structural understanding.

Now what if this "digital materiality" were to transcend the scale of an individual wall element? What if larger inhabitable structures—or even entire cities—were developed according to such design principles? What if mechanization once again took command? RETO GEISER

HEART OF BRICKS
PAVILION FOR GALLERY SEROUSSI, PARIS, COMPETITION 2007

The Seroussi Pavilion is conceived as a single-storey glass house, enclosing a "heart of brick." The role of this masonry core, which consists of a series of curvilinear, alternately transparent, solid, expressive or calm, digitally fabricated brick walls, is dual: it provides the structural core of the building, supporting the cantilever of the roof on all sides, while constituting a complex spatial device. Its concave sides create a generous enfilade of varying spaces, which unfurls along the glass façade of the pavilion, generating multiple views of the surrounding park and beyond to Paris.

On the convex side, the walls combine to form an introverted central core, which contains the building's infrastructure: kitchen, sanitary and storage rooms as well as a space for viewing video art. The core is covered by a concrete roof that is "draped" over the walls through a simulation of gravitational forces, creating a complex, double-curved surface.

A series of individually oriented skylights puncture this surface, channeling proper lighting where necessary, providing selective views of the neighboring sculptural tower by André Bloc, and creating an atmosphere of dappled light that refers to the canopy of tree leaves in the park outside. Seen from the tower, this sculpted, perforated roof constitutes a fifth façade, revealing the building's internal forms and organization.

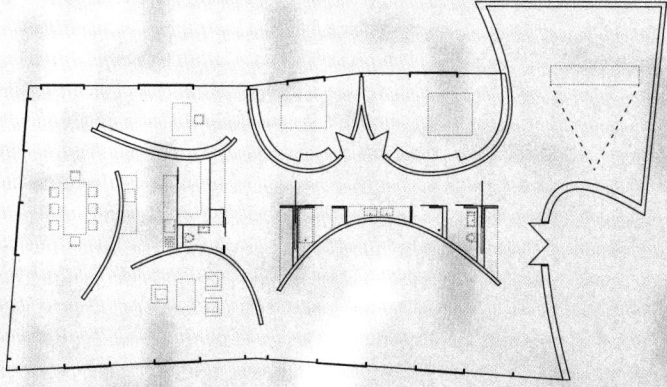

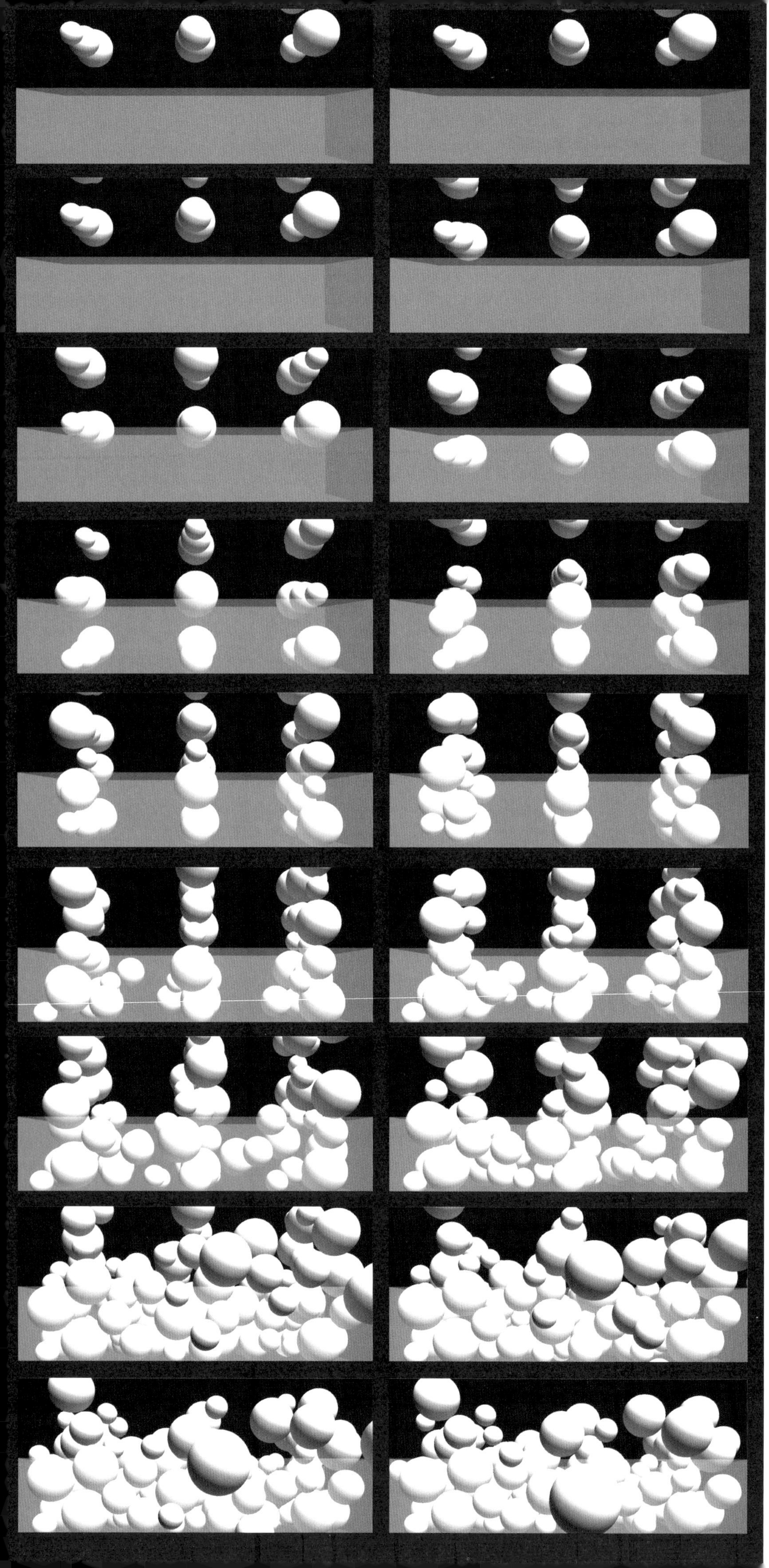

17° OF DEVIATION

GANTENBEIN VINEYARD FAÇADE, FLÄSCH, 2006
In cooperation with Bearth & Deplazes Architects. Clients: Martha and Daniel Gantenbein

FALLING SPHERES. To create the façade, we designed a generation process which interpreted the concrete frame construction by Bearth & Deplazes as a basket and filled it with abstract, oversized grapes of varying diameters. We digitally simulated gravity to make the grapes fall into this virtual basket, until they were closely packed. Then we viewed the result from all four sides and transferred the digital image data to the rotation of the individual bricks. On the built façades, the visitor discerns gigantic, synthetic grapes, which were virtually inside the building as we developed our design.

However, the architectural implications of this brick façade are more elaborate and diverse than those of a two-dimensional image. To the human eye, able to detect even the finest difference in color and lightness, the subtle deflection of the bricks creates an appearance and plasticity that is constantly changing along with the movement of the observer and of the sun over the course of the day.

The joints between the bricks were left open to create transparency and allow daylight to trickle into the building. In order to make the pattern discernible from the interior we laid the bricks as close together as possible so that the gap at full deflection was nearly closed. This produced a maximum contrast between the open and the closed joints and allowed the light to model the interior walls poetically.

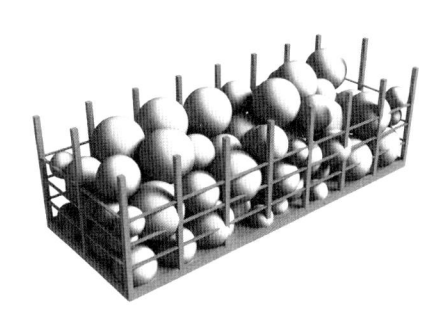

The project was realized as an extension of a small but remarkably successful vineyard. The wine producers wanted a new service building, consisting of a large fermentation room for processing grapes, a cellar dug into the ground for storing the wine barrels, and a roof terrace for wine tastings and receptions. Bearth & Deplazes Architects designed the project, and it was already under construction when they invited us to design its façade.

The initial design proposed a simple concrete skeleton filled with bricks: the masonry acts as a temperature buffer, as well as filtering the sunlight for the fermentation room behind it. The bricks are offset in such a way that daylight penetrates the hall through the gaps between the bricks. Direct sunlight, which would have a detrimental effect on the fermentation, is however excluded. Polycarbonate panels are mounted inside to protect against wind. On the upper floor, the bricks form the balustrade of the roof terrace.

The robotic production method that we developed at the ETH enabled us to lay each one of the 20,000 bricks precisely according to programmed parameters—at the desired angle and at the exact prescribed intervals. This allowed us to design and construct each wall to possess the desired light and air permeability, while creating a pattern that covers the entire building façades. According to the angle at which they are set, the individual bricks each reflect light differently and thus take on different degrees of lightness. Similarly to pixels on a computer screen they add up to a distinctive image and thus communicate the identity of the vineyard. In contrast to a two-dimensional screen, however, there is a dramatic play between plasticity, depth and color, dependent on the viewer's position and the angle of the sun.

The masonry of the vineyard's façade looks like an enormous basket filled with grapes. At closer view—in contrast to its pictorial effect at a distance—the sensual, textile softness of the walls dissolves into the materiality of the stonework. The observer is surprised that the soft, round forms are actually composed of individual, hard bricks. The façade appears as a solidified dynamic form, in whose three-dimensional depth the viewer's eye is invited to wander. In the interior, the daylight that penetrates creates a mild, yet luminous atmosphere. Looking towards the light, the design becomes manifest in its modulation through the open gaps. It is superimposed on the image of the landscape that glimmers through at different levels of definition according to the perceived contrast.

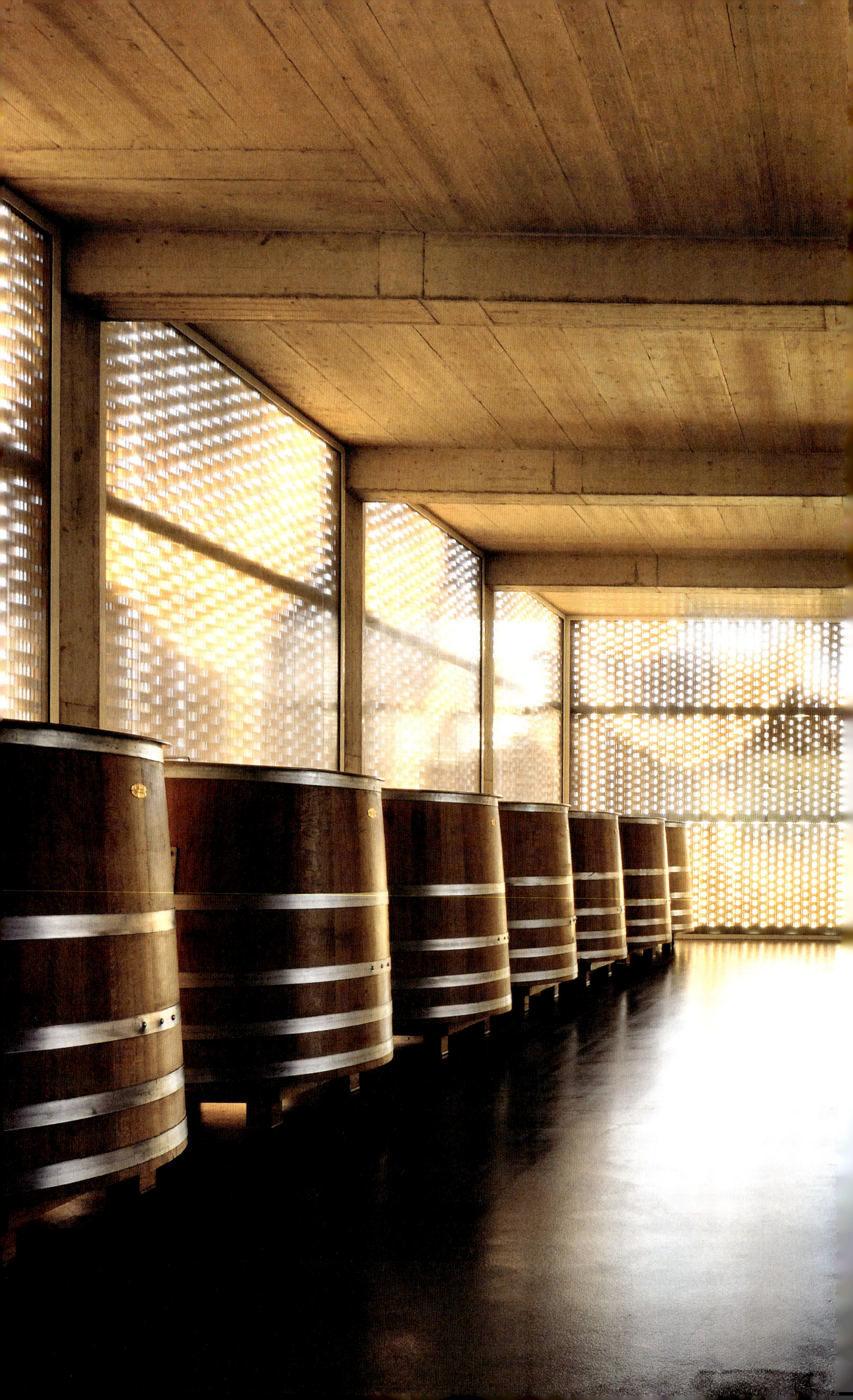

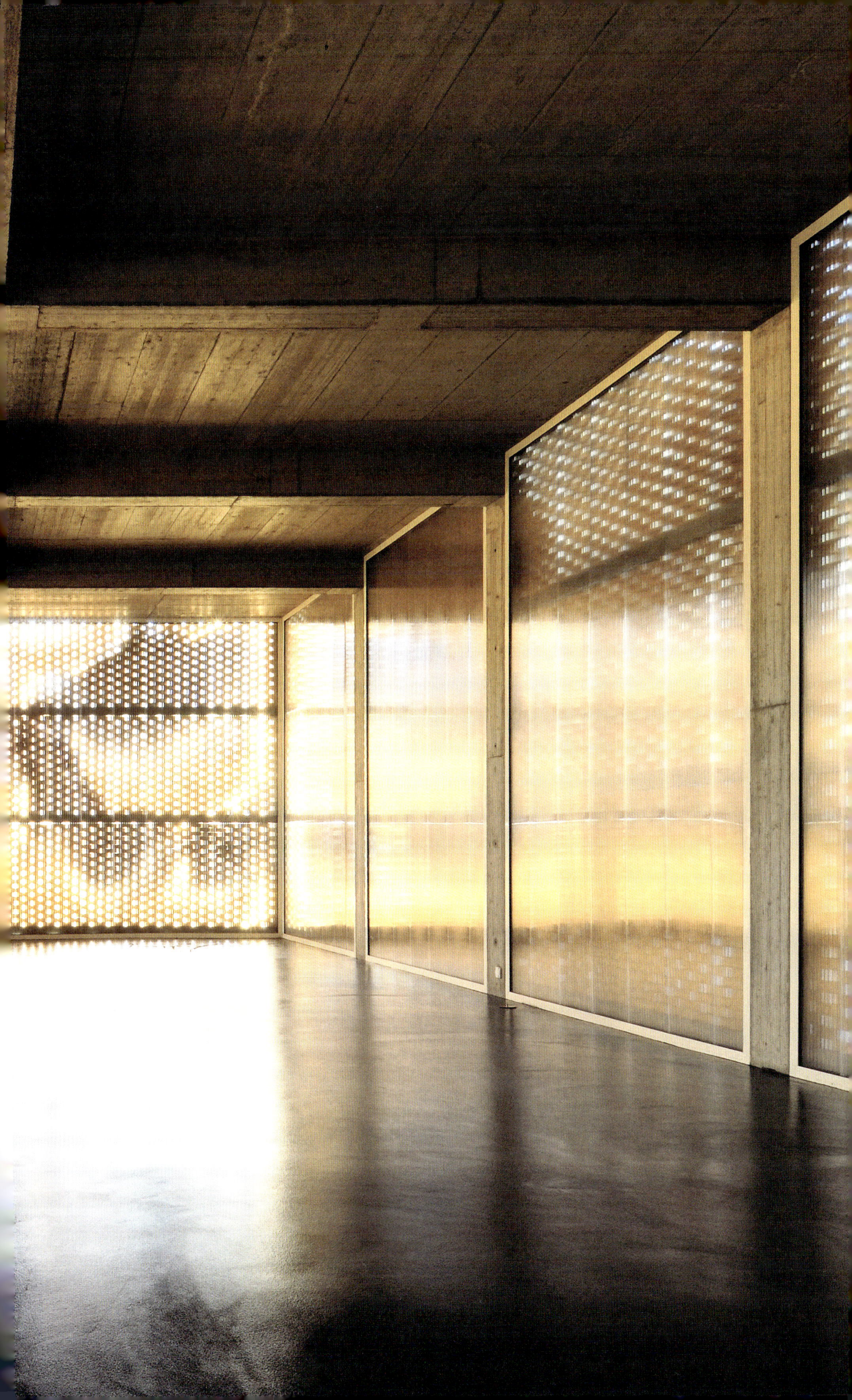

BRICKLAYING. The wall elements were manufactured as a pilot project in our research facilities at the ETH Zurich, transported by lorry to the construction site, and installed using a crane. Because construction was already quite advanced, we had only three months before assembly on site. This made manufacturing the seventy-two façade elements a challenge both technologically and in terms of deadlines. As the robot could be driven directly by the design data, without our having to produce additional implementation drawings, we were able to work on the design of the façade up to the very last minute before starting production.

To accelerate the manufacturing process for the 400 square meter façade, we had to develop an automated process for applying the two-component bonding agent. Because each brick has a different rotation, every single brick has a different and unique overlap with the brick below it, and the one below that. Together with the brick manufacturer's engineer, we established a method in which four parallel bonding agent paths are applied, for each brick individually, at predefined intervals to the central axis of the wall element. Load tests performed on the first elements manufactured revealed that the bonding agent was so structurally effective that the reinforcement normally required for conventional prefabricated walls was unnecessary.

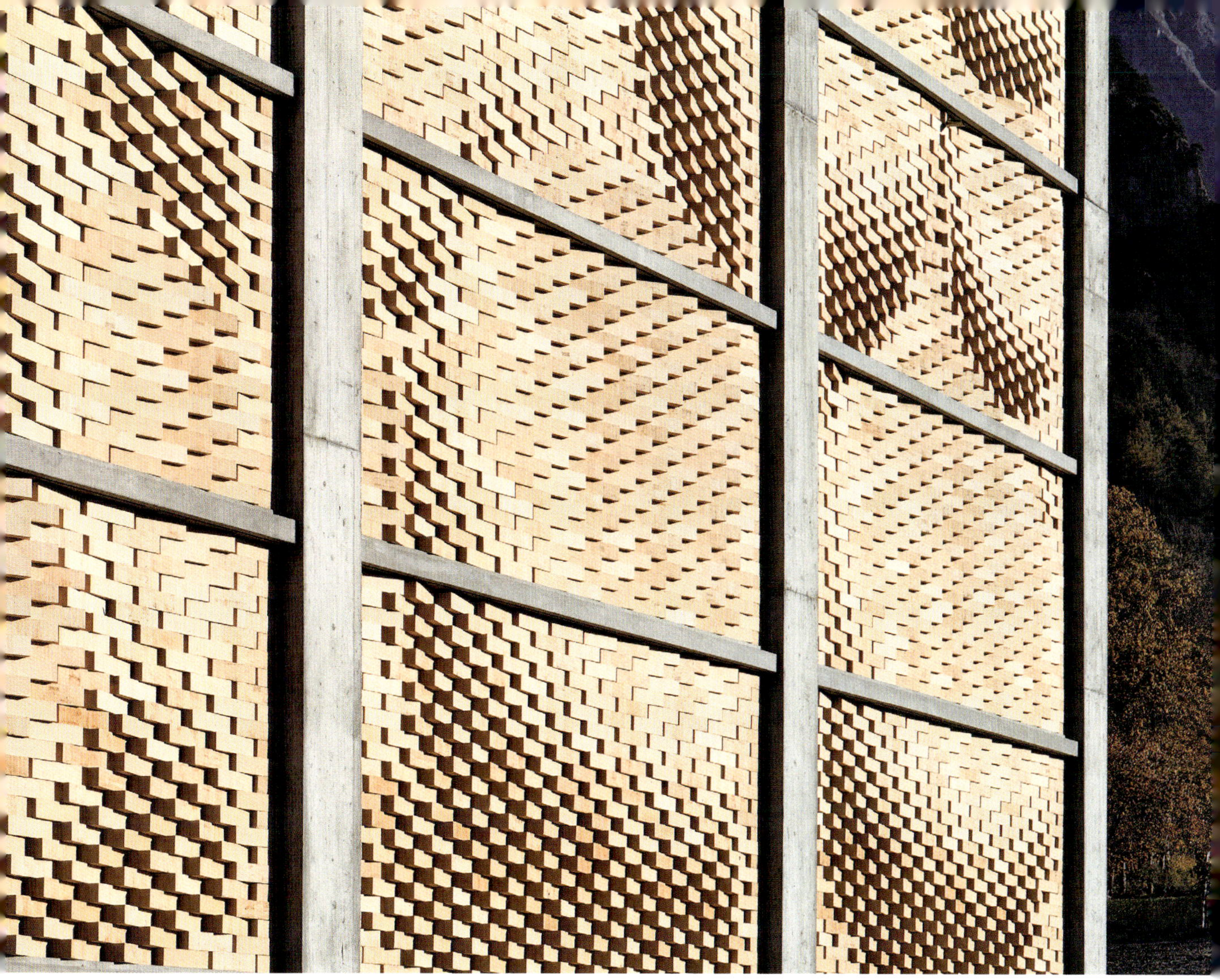

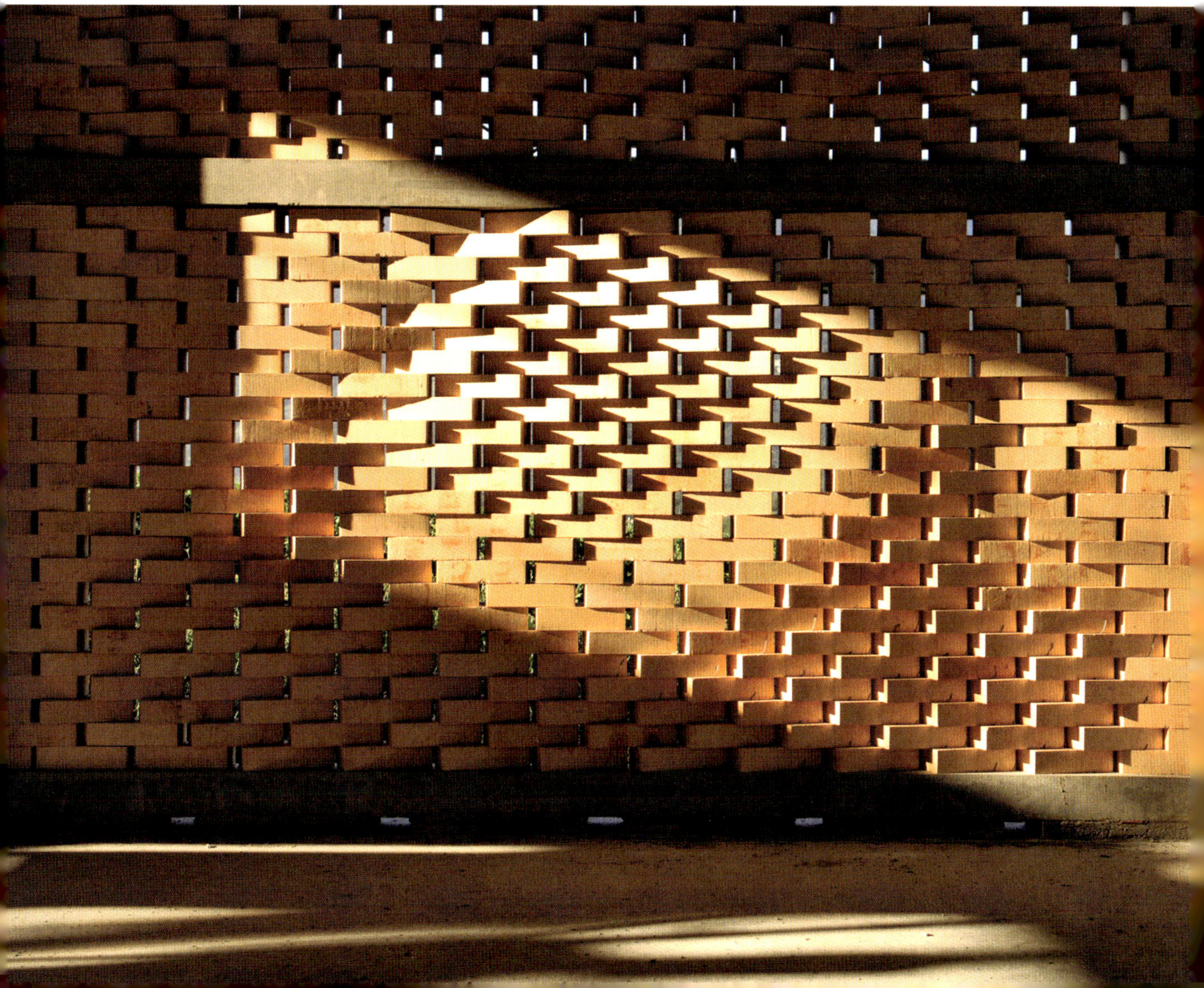

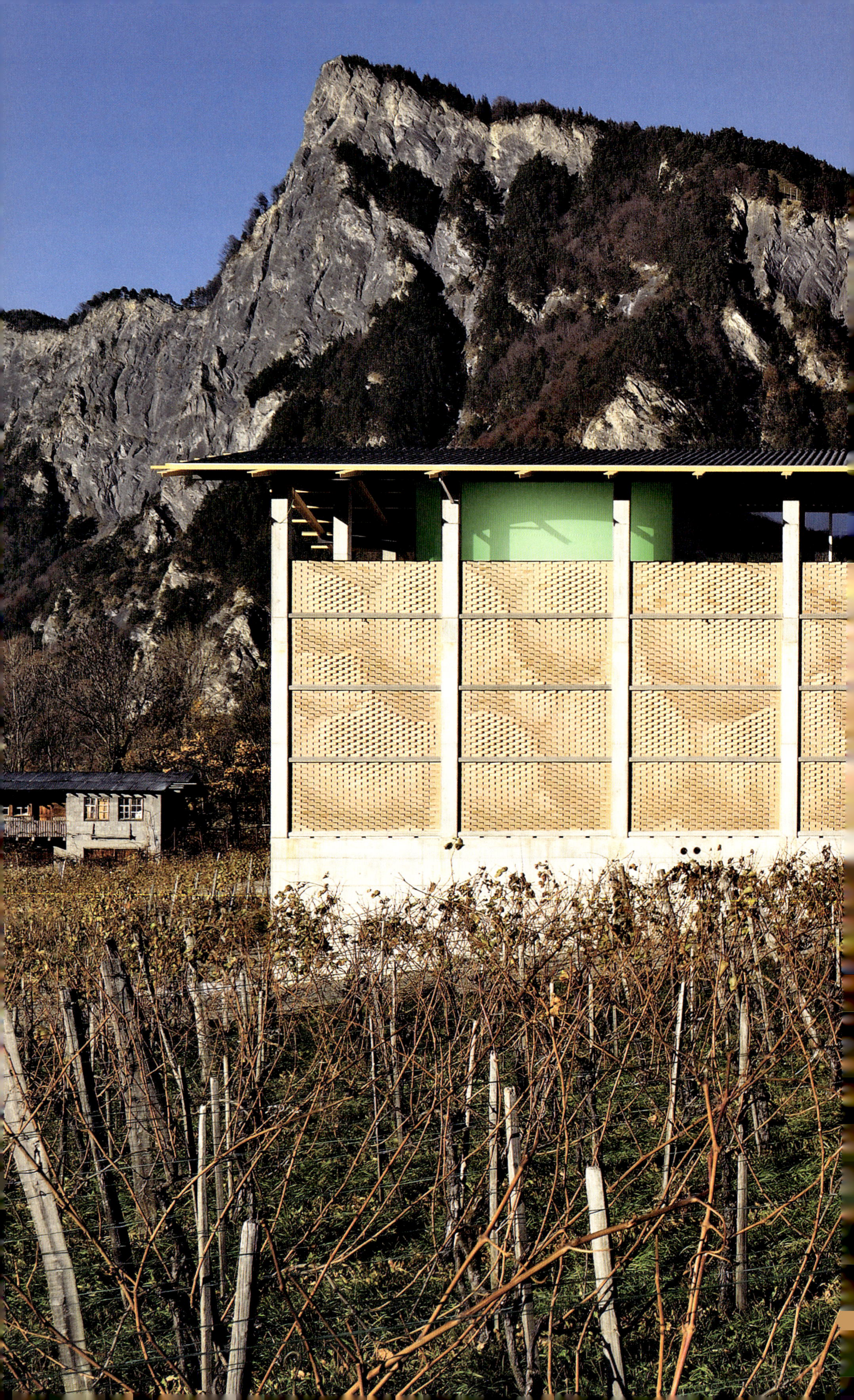

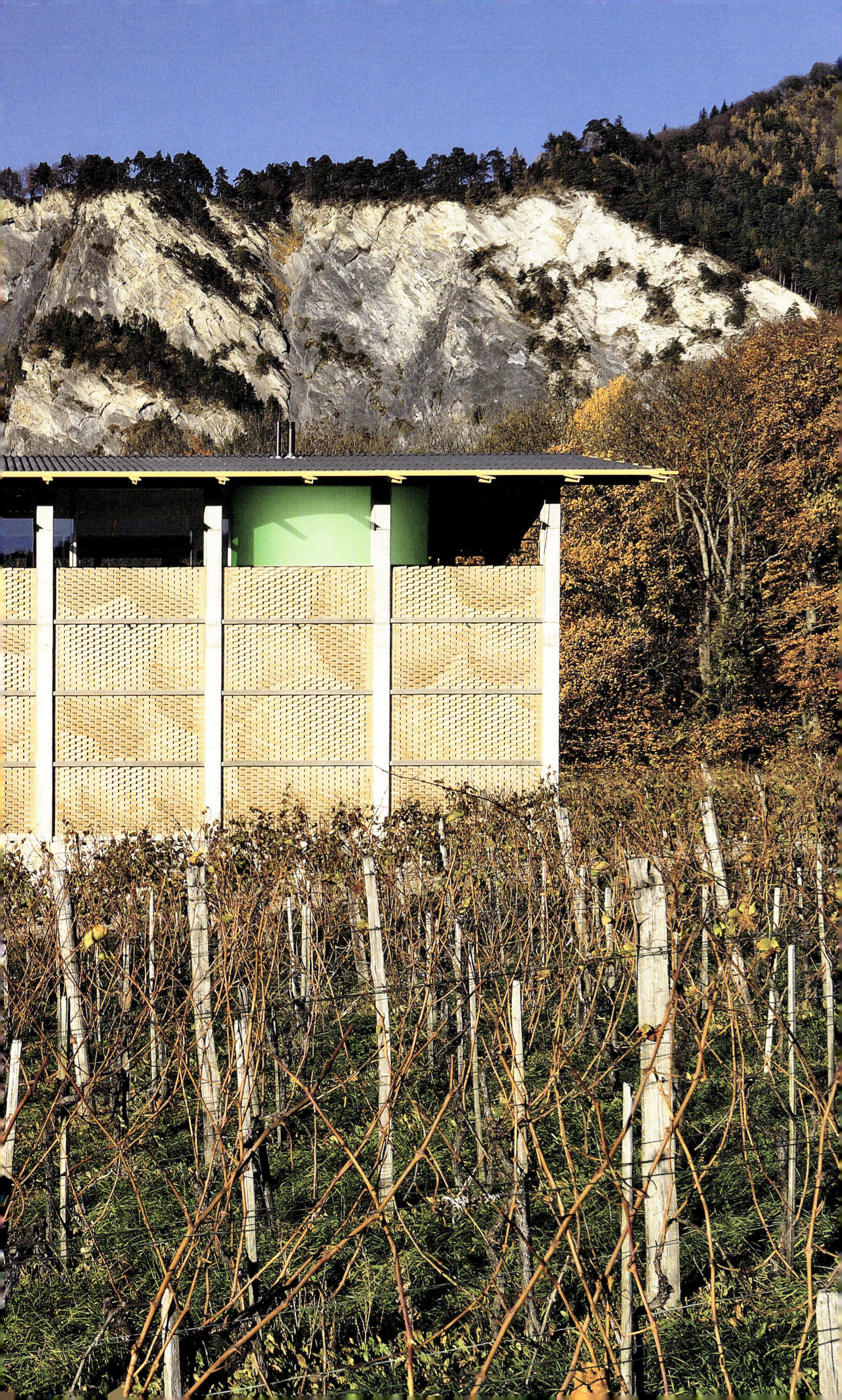

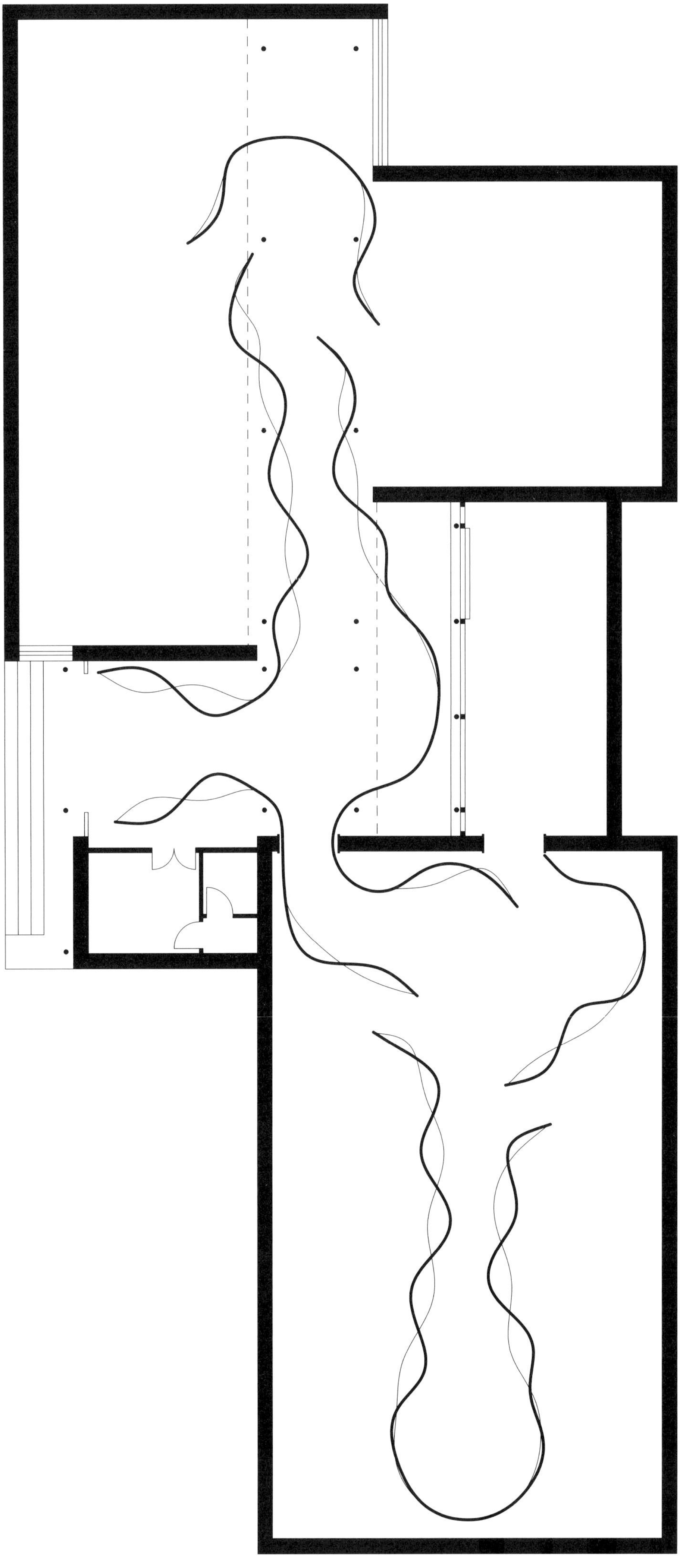

STRUCTURAL OSCILLATIONS

INSTALLATION AT THE 11TH VENICE ARCHITECTURE BIENNALE, SWISS PAVILION, 2008
In cooperation with: Reto Geiser, Curator. Client: Swiss Federal Office of Culture

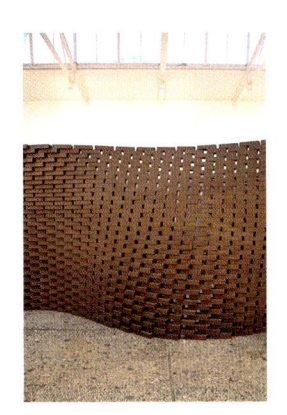

For the exhibition "Explorations" about contemporary methods of design research in architecture, we designed a 100-meter-long brick wall that runs as a continuous ribbon through the Swiss pavilion.

The wall installation was built on site at the Giardini, the grounds of the Biennale in Venice, by the R-O-B mobile robotic fabrication unit. The wall's looped form defined an involuted, central space within the existing pavilion, from which the visitor was able to access the interstitial exhibition spaces generated between wall and pavilion. Through its materiality and spatial configuration, the wall, which consisted of 14,961 individually rotated bricks, entered into a direct dialogue with the modernist brick structure from 1951 by Swiss architect Bruno Giacometti.

The wall's design was conceived as a system with open parameters. The path of a single, continuous curve carried all the generative information necessary to define the design. This curve functioned as a conceptual interface between the curator and us. It allowed us to negotiate the needs of the individual research groups' exhibitions and to iteratively generate a layout that matched these spatial requirements right up to the moment of production.

The three-dimensional, plastic wall was automatically generated after each modification of the generative curve. Its complex shape was determined by the constructive requirement that each single, 4-meter-long segment of wall should be structurally independent of the rest. Where the path of the generative curve was almost straight, meaning that the elements could easily be toppled over by the visitors, the wall's footprint took on a sinusoidal form, thus increasing its stability. Each curvature in the lower layers was balanced by a counter-curvature in the upper layers, thus giving the wall its architectural expression. The wall loop's shape varied along its path, widening and narrowing, producing spaces rich in tension, which led the visitors through the exhibition. In addition, by rotating individual bricks according to the curvature, we generated the surface texture of the wall: the more crooked the line, the greater the rotation of the bricks. This further emphasized the wall's plastic deformation, which acquired an almost textile character, in pulsating contrast to the firm materiality of the bricks.

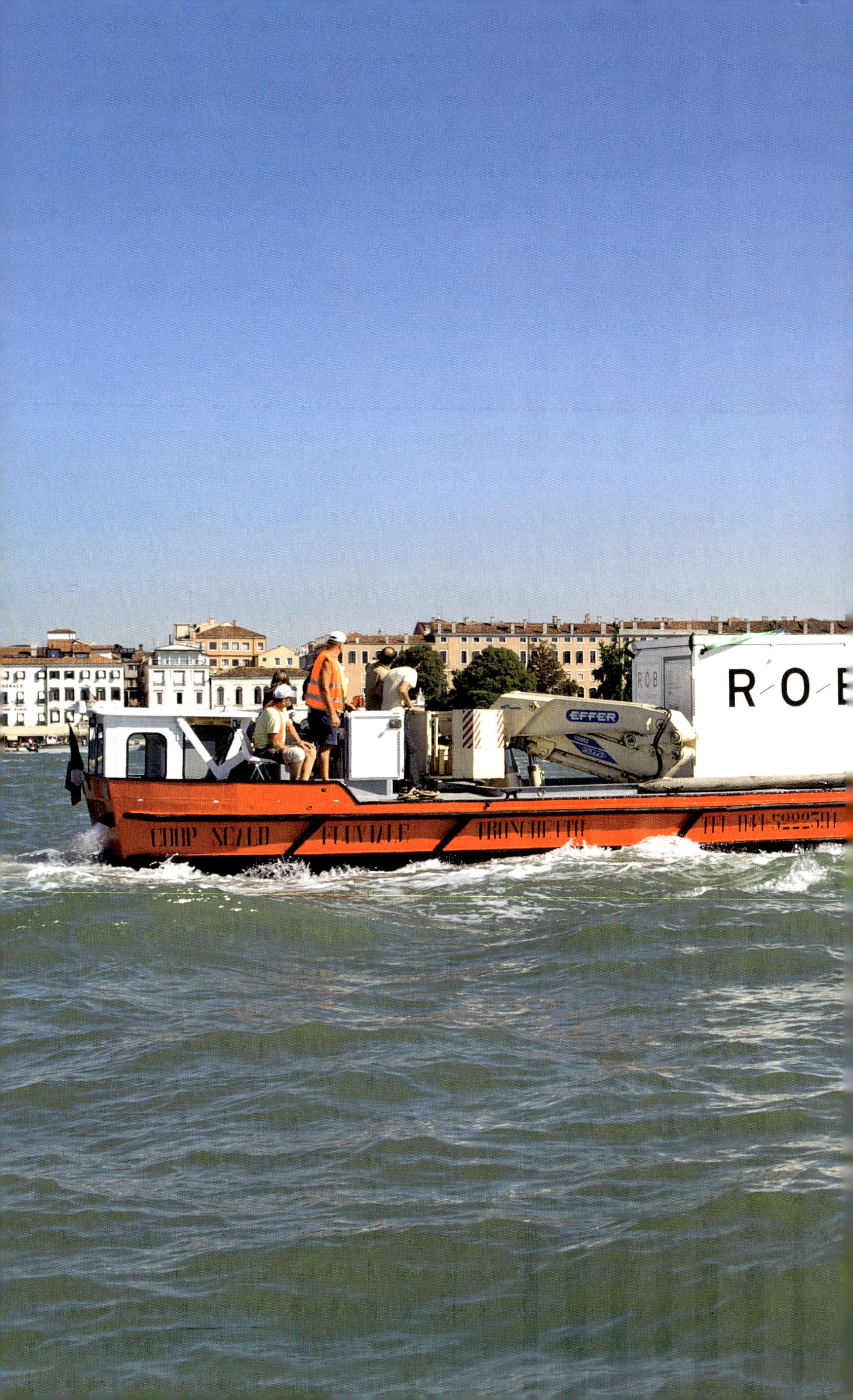

R O B
EFFER
COOP SCALO
FLUVIALE
TRONCHETTO

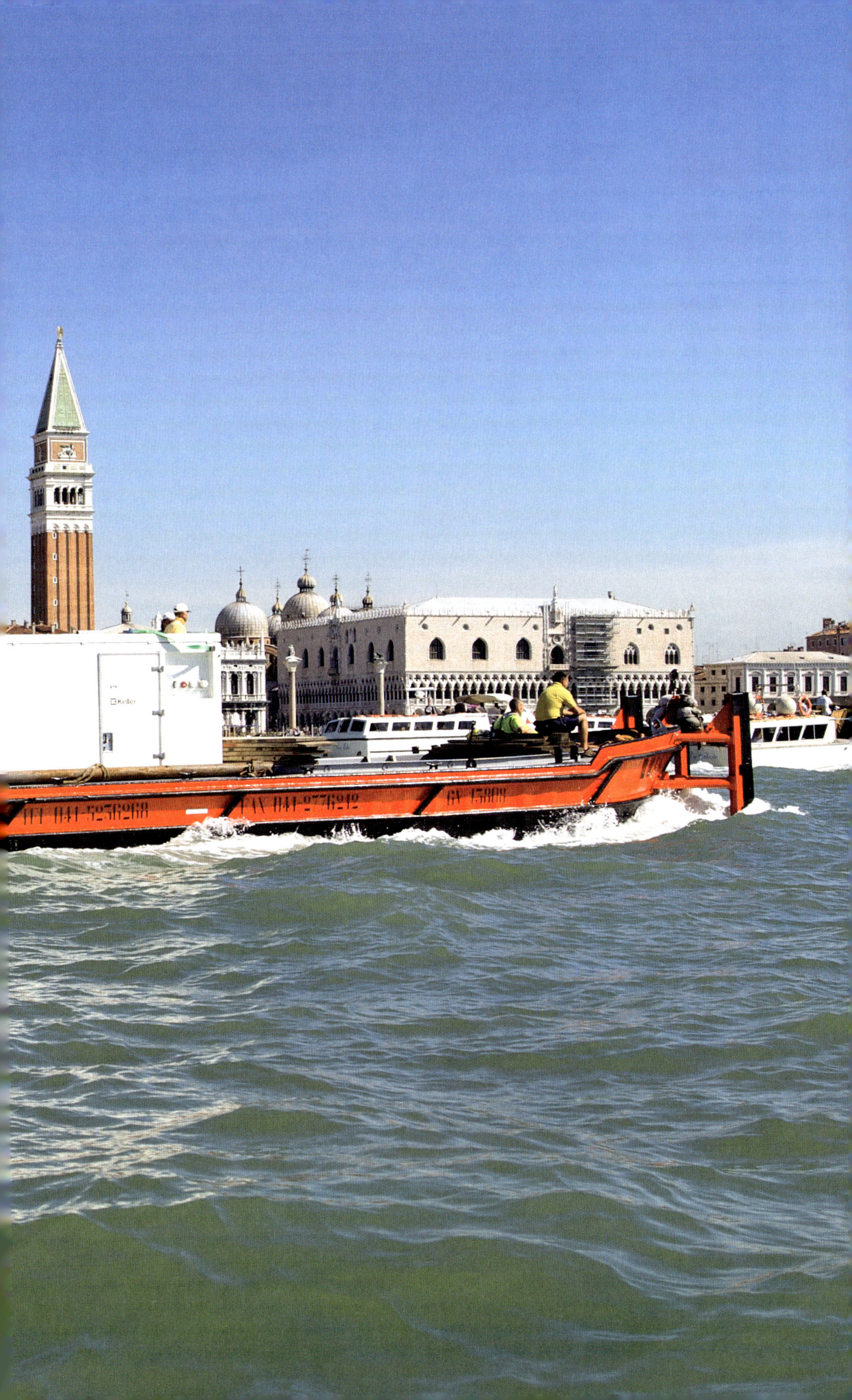

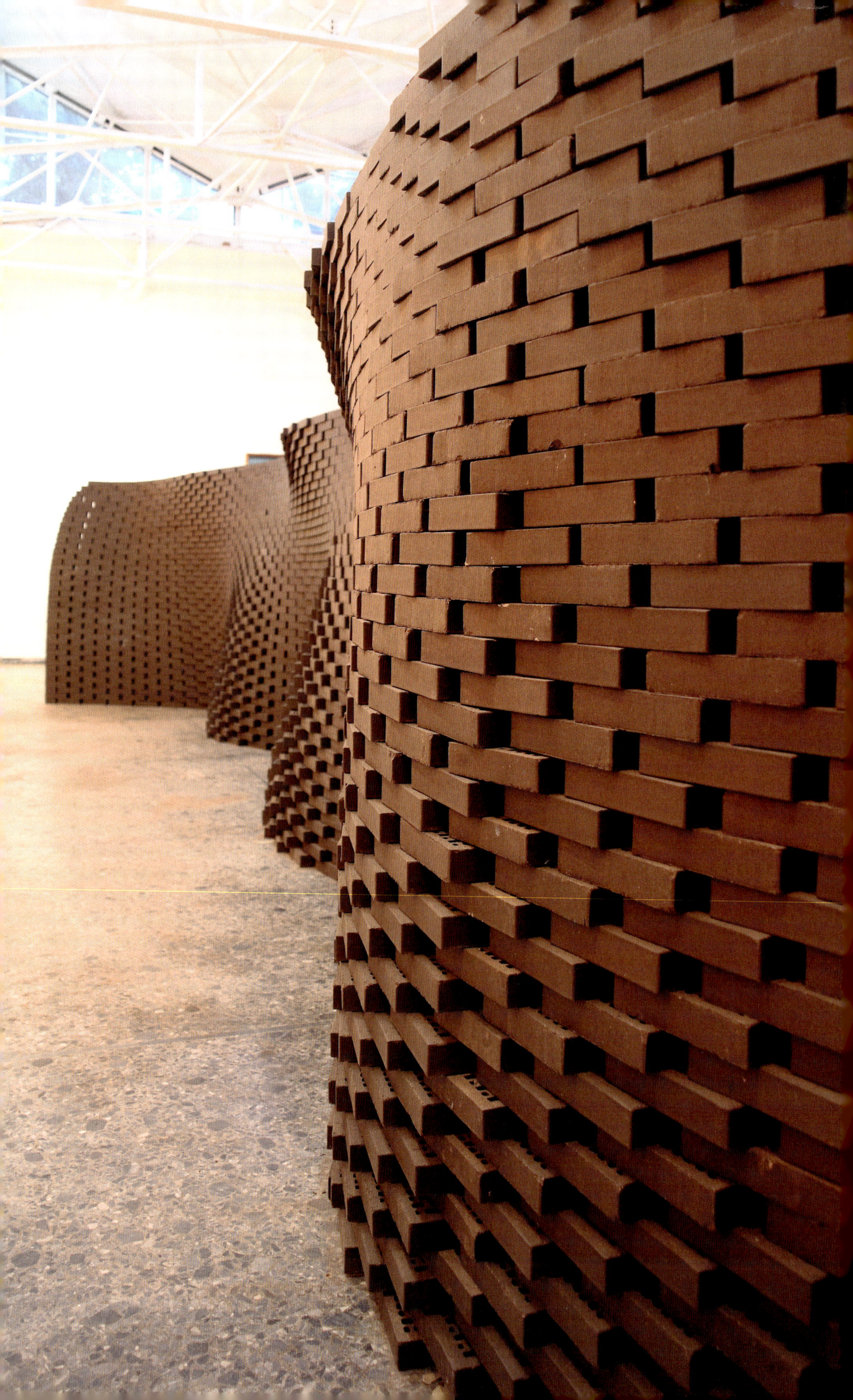

107

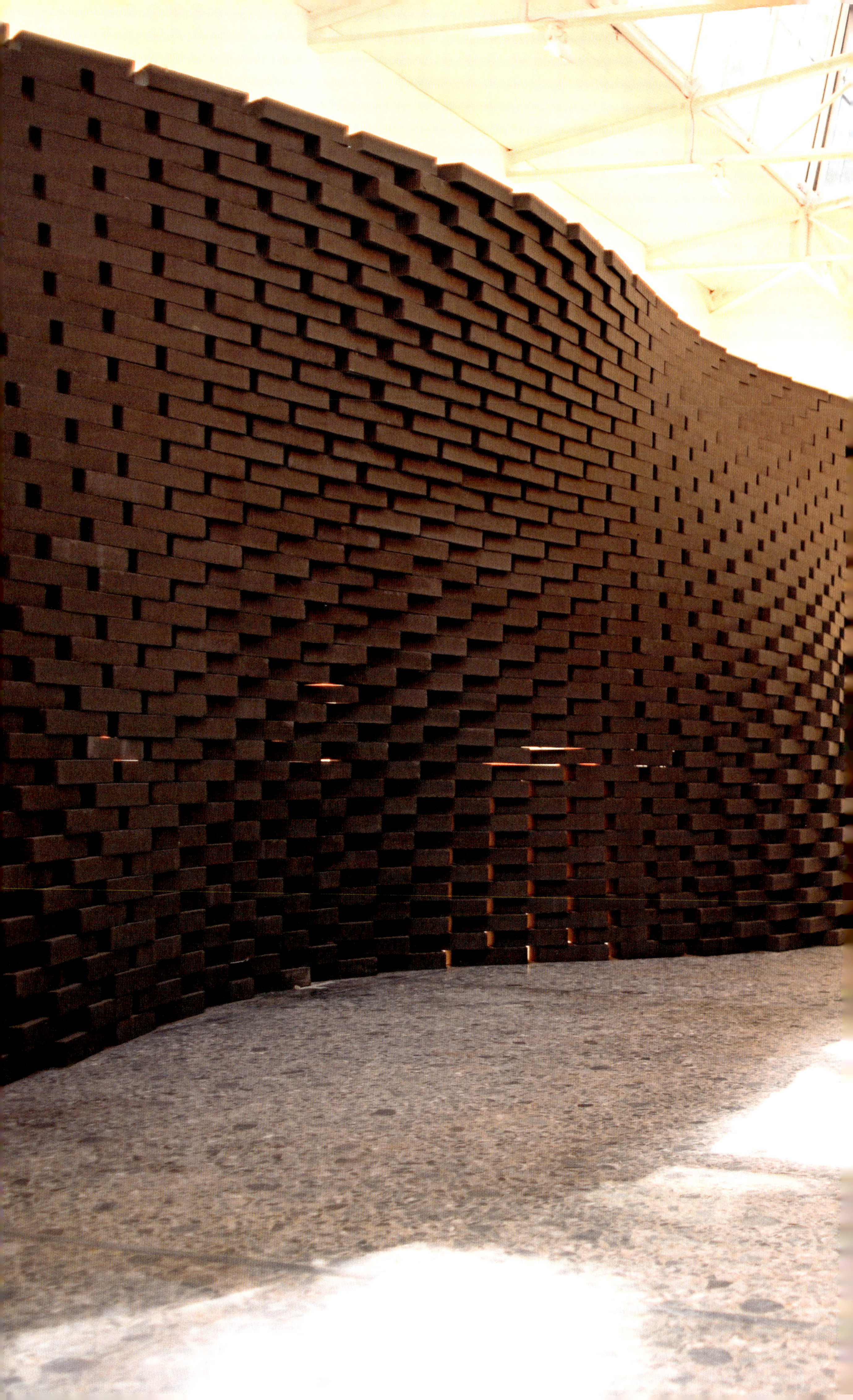

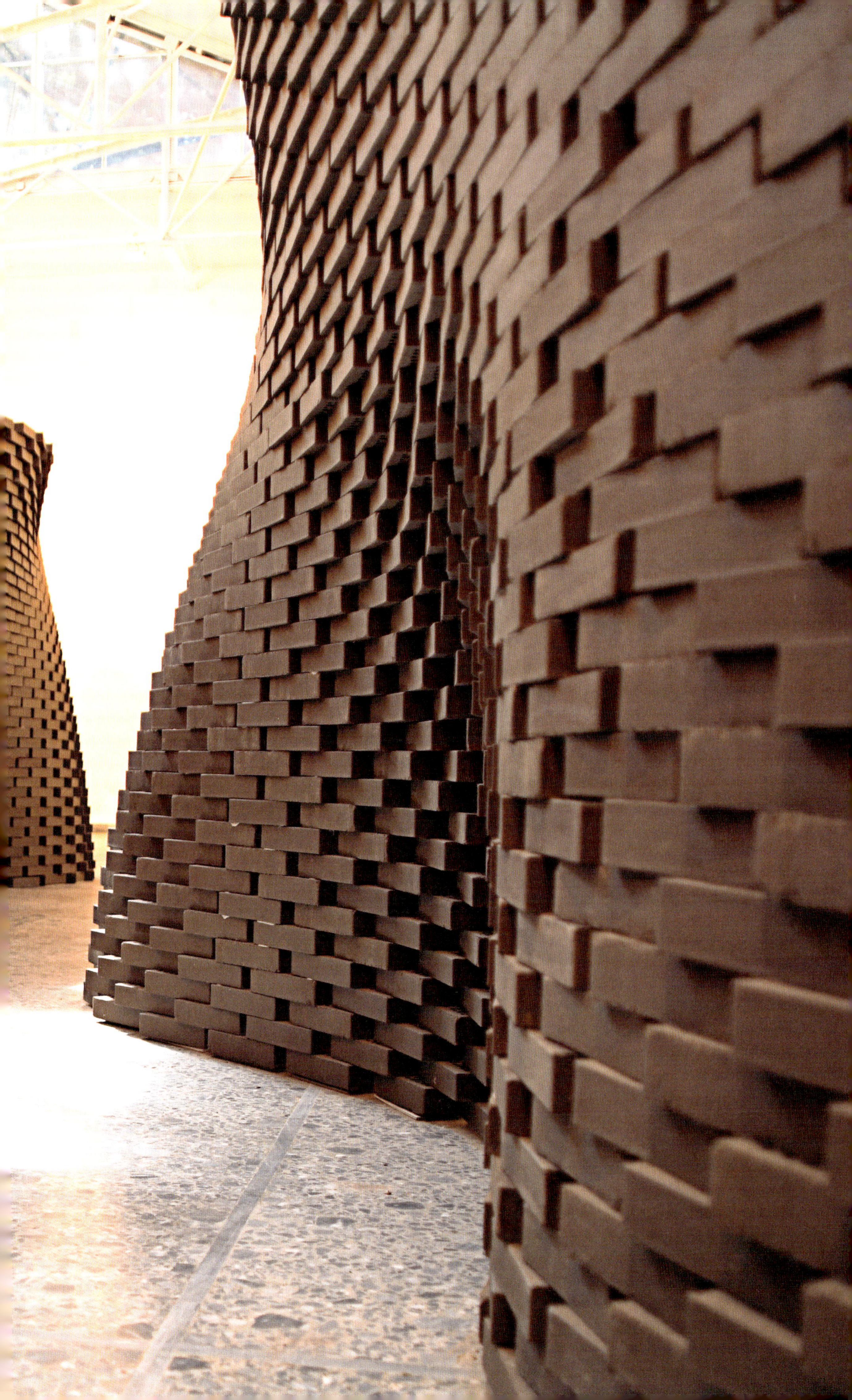

COLLABORATORS 2000–2008

Office: Ralph Bärtschi, Tobias Bonwetsch, Beat Ferrario, Raffael Gaus, Rasmus Joergensen, Rotraut Kager, Michael Knauss, Thomas Melliger, Anja Meyer, Silvan Oesterle, Pino Pavese, Markus Schietsch, Odilo Schoch, Marc Schwarz, Patrick Sibenaler, Christian Verasani. Interns: Patrick Achermann, Manuel Bader, Damaris Baumann, Boris Gusic, Raphaela Hurscheler, Claudia Nasri, Vanessa Neukirch, Michael Oswald, Sascha Robert, Thomas Summermatter

ETH Zurich: Ralph Bärtschi, Tobias Bonwetsch, Michael Hanak, Jan-Henrik Hansen, Michael Knauss, Daniel Kobel, Michael Lyrenmann, Silvan Oesterle. Teaching assistants: Daniel Abraha, Stephan Achermann, Ladina Esslinger, Boris Gusic, Katrin Hasler, Kasper Hofer, Christoph Junk, Andri Lüscher, Hannes Oswald, Martin Kostelezky, Lukas Pauer, Chantal Reichenbach, Martin Tann, Frank Thesseling

PROJECT CREDITS

mTable (see page 12 ff)
Collaborators: Beat Ferrario, Patrick Sibenaler
Selected experts: Thomas Killer (communication), Viola Zimmermann (graphic design)
Partners: CNC Dynamix, superform, SwissHolz

Centro Balneare (see page 16 f)
Collaborators: Boris Gusic (project leader), Silvan Oesterle, Miriam Weber

Interference Cube (see page 18 ff)
Partners: CNC Dynamix, Jura Cement, Wey Elementbau

Monte Rosa Alpine Hut (see page 22 f)
In cooperation with: Studio Monte Rosa ETH Zurich
Client: Swiss Alpine Club SAC
Collaborators: Tobias Bonwetsch (project leader), Ralph Bärtschi

sWISH* (see page 24 ff)
Scenography: Morphing Systems and Miriam Zehnder
Collaborators: Beat Ferrario (project leader), Rasmus Joergensen, Odilo Schoch, Patrick Sibenaler
Selected experts: SJB + Partner (Structural engineering), Rolf Derrer (lighting), Preti Haustechnik (natural cooling)
Selected contractors: AGF (polyurethane skin), CNC Dynamix (milling)

Private House (see page 30 f)
Collaborators: Raffael Gaus (project leader), Anya Meyer, Cristian Verasani, Manuel Bader, Damaris Baumann, Claudia Nasri, Silvan Oesterle
Selected experts: Thomas Melliger (building planning), Reto Ambass (structural engineering), Raumanzug (building physics)

Tanzhaus (see page 34 ff)
In cooperation with: blue architects, Zurich
Collaborators: Thomas Melliger (project leader), Thomas Hildebrand, Pino Pavese, Miriam Seiler, Massimo Della Corte, Reto Giovanoli, Boris Gusic, Raphaela Hurschler, Miriam Weber
Selected experts: Volkert & Zimmermann (structural engineering), Strauss Elektroakustik (room acoustics), Rolf Derrer (lighting), Mebatech (façade glazing)

Lightline (see page 40 f)
Client: City of Uster
Selected experts: Atelier Derrer (lighting), Ralph Bärtschi (lighting programming), sibenaler mca (programming)

Bahnhofstrasse Christmas Lights (see page 42 ff)
Collaborators: Marc Schwarz, Patrick Sibenaler, Damaris Baumann, Claudia Nasri
Selected experts: Arup (structural engineering), Arup Lighting (lighting consulting), Rolf Derrer (lighting consulting)
Selected contractors: ims (lighting), Cowex (filament winding), Kummler + Matter (cable structure)

R-O-B (see page 57 ff)
In cooperation with: Keller Ziegeleien
Collaborators: Michael Lyrenmann (project leader), Tobias Bonwetsch
Selected contractors: Bachmann Engineering (integration), Viola Zimmermann (corporate identity)

The Programmed Wall (see page 62 f)
Collaborators: Tobias Bonwetsch (project leader), Daniel Kobel, Michael Lyrenmann
Students: Matthias Buehler, Michael Knauss, Leon Kocan, Silvan Oesterle, Goncales Manteigas, Dominik Sigg
Partner: Keller Ziegeleien

Domoterra Lounge (see page 62)
Collaborators: Tobias Bonwetsch (project leader), Daniel Kobel, Michael Lyrenmann
Students: Philipp Bollier, Robin Budel, Daniel Cajöri, Ursina Götz, Maria Imbach, Georg Krummenacher, Daniel Lütolf, Florian Stroh, Thomas Summermatter, Matthias Thaler
Partners: Domoterra, Keller Ziegeleien, StauffacherBenz

The Resolution Wall (see page 64 f)
Collaborators: Tobias Bonwetsch (project leader), Ralph Bärtschi, Daniel Kobel, Michael Lyrenmann
Students: Marcia Akermann, Gregor Bieri, Stefan Bischof, Eliza Boganski, Philip Braem, Frank-Olivier Cottier, Irene Lo Iacono, Andreas Kast
Partner: Ytong

Foam (see page 66 ff)
Collaborators: Silvan Oesterle (project leader), Ralph Bärtschi, Michael Lyrenmann
Students: Christian Blasimann, Elisa Brusky, Kathrin Hasler, Daniel Hässig, Nils Havelka, Andres Herzog, Kaspar Hofer, Jacob Jansen, Bettina Jochum, Christoph Junk, Yuta Kanezuka, Simon Kraus, Hannes Oswald, Christoph Rauhut, Michael Reiterer, Sibèlle Urben, Aline Vuilliomenet, Philipp Zimmer, Barbara Zwicky
Selected experts: Jürgen Strauss (acoustics), Kurt Eggenschwiler, EMPA (acoustics)
Partner: CellForm, PU-Technik Meier

The Sequential Wall (see page 70 ff)
Collaborators: Silvan Oesterle (project leader), Ralph Bärtschi, Michael Lyrenmann
Students: Michael Bühler, Clarence Chia Tien San, David Dalsass, Ramirez Daniel, Simon Filler, Milena Isler, Roman Kallweit, Morten Krog, Ellen Leuenberger, Daniel Lütolf, Jonas Nauwelaertz de Agé, Jonathan Roider, Steffen Samberger, Andre Schmid, Chantal Thomet, Rafael Venetz, Pascal Waldburger, Nik Werenfels, Libei Zhao
Partner: Häring Holz- und Systembau

The Oblique Hole (see page 78 f)
Collaborators: Jan-Henrik Hansen (project leader), Tobias Bonwetsch, Daniel Kobel, Michael Lyrenmann
Students: Christian Beerli, Matthias Bernhard, Matthias Bühler, Mauro Caviezel, Oliver Dibrova, Francis Fawcett, Stefan Förg, Raffael Gaus, Matthias Heberle, Michael Hirschbichler, Evert Klinkenberg, Michael Knauss, Léonard Kocan, Matthias Milan Kulstrunk, Mark Lauener, Barbara Leonardi, Lorenz Leuenberger, Gonçalo Manteigas, David Thomas Mathyl, Lucius Meyer, Silvan Oesterle, Natalie Pomer, Patrick Schneider, Dominik Sigg, Lukas Sonderegger, Valeria Tarkhova, Lorenz Weingart

The Perforated Wall (see page 80 ff)
Collaborators: Daniel Kobel (project leader), Patrick Stähli (IFB), Ralph Bärtschi, Michael Lyrenmann
Students: Sasha Cicar, Natalia Dorta, Ladina Esslinger, Philip Eversmann, Sabrina Gehrig, Chris Keller, Florian Poppele, Stefan Rohrer, Willy Stähelin, Michael Walton, Melanie Weidmann, Lorenz Weingart, Xu Zhang
Selected expert: Patrick Stähli, IFB ETH Zurich (concrete)
Partners: Geberit, Holzco-Doka, Holcim, Swisspor

The Dissolved Wall (see page 86 f)
Collaborators: Daniel Kobel (project leader), Ralph Bärtschi, Michael Lyrenmann
Students: Philip Bräm, Kai Franz, Georg Krummenacher, Andri Lüscher, Daniel Lütolf, Ivo Piazza, Alexandr Prusakov, Christoph Rauhut, Thomas Summermatter, Mulan Sun, Darryl Trotter
Selected experts: Urs Roth (geometry)
Partner: Swisspor

Science City Construction Hoarding (see page 86)
Collaborators: Daniel Kobel (project leader), Ralph Bärtschi, Michael Lyrenmann
Students: Ania Apolinarska, Gregor Bieri, Stefan Bischof, Reto Gsell, Christoph Hefti, Sandra Lentes, Armin Roost, Nadine Schütz
Partner: KCAP Architects & Planners, Science City / ETH Zurich,

Science City Housing (see page 88 f)
Collaborators: Raffael Gaus (project leader), Manuel Bader, Ralph Bärtschi, Tobias Bonwetsch
Selected experts: Schweingruber Zulauf (landscape architecture), Dr. Lüchinger & Meyer (structural engineering), Raumanzug (building physics), Archobau (costs), Gerald Orick and Prof. Dr. Stevenson University of Tennessee (circle packing façade),

Pavilion for Gallery Seroussi (see page 92 f)
Collaborators: Tobias Bonwetsch (project leader), Georg Krummenacher, Daniel Lütolf, Susanne Mocek, David Ritz, Thomas Summermatter, Miriam Weber
Selected expert: vi.vo.maria viñe.martina voser. (landscape architecture)

Gantenbein Vineyard Façade (see page 94 ff)
In cooperation with: Bearth & Deplazes Architects, Valentin Bearth, Andrea Deplazes, Daniel Ladner, Chur/Zurich
Collaborators: Tobias Bonwetsch (project leader), Michael Knauss, Michael Lyrenmann, Silvan Oesterle, Daniel Abraha, Stephan Achermann, Christoph Junk, Andri Lüscher, Martin Tann
Selected experts: Jürg Buchli (structural engineering), Dr. Nebojsa Mojsilovic and Markus Baumann, IBK ETH Zurich (load bearing tests)
Partner: Keller Ziegeleien

Venice Architecture Biennale (see page 102 ff)
In cooperation with: Reto Geiser (curator)
Collaborators: Michael Knauss (project leader), Tobias Bonwetsch, Michael Lyrenmann, Ralph Bärtschi, Gregor Bieri, Michael Bühler, Hannes Oswald, Lukas Pauer
Partner: Keller Ziegeleien, KUKA Robotics, Sika

FABIO GRAMAZIO (1970) received his degree in architecture from the Swiss Federal Institute of Technology (ETH Zurich) in 1996. From 1996 to 2000 he was a scientific collaborator at ETH Zurich with Professor Gerhard Schmitt. He is a co-founder of the art collective *etoy*, which has been active since 1994.

Since 2000 Fabio Gramazio and Matthias Kohler have been joint partners in the Zurich architecture and urbanism practice Gramazio & Kohler. Their award-winning works include the *Gantenbein* vineyard façade, the *Tanzhaus* theatre for contemporary dance, the Christmas lights for the *Bahnhofstrasse* in Zurich and the *sWISH** Pavilion at the Swiss National Exposition *Expo.02*.

Since 2005 Fabio Gramazio and Matthias Kohler have been assistant professors of *Architecture and Digital Fabrication* at the ETH Zurich Faculty of Architecture. Their research and teaching focus on architectural design strategies for full-scale robotic fabrication. Highly informed architectural elements are explored for their sensual, constructive and economic potential. They initiated the first robotic research lab in 2005 and the first transportable robotic unit for on-site fabrication in 2008.

MATTHIAS KOHLER (1968) received his degree in architecture from the Swiss Federal Institute of Technology (ETH Zurich) in 1996. He was a scientific collaborator at ETH Zurich with Professor Marc Angélil from 1997 to 1998 and with Professor Greg Lynn from 1999 to 2000.

Since 2000 Matthias Kohler and Fabio Gramazio have been joint partners in the Zurich architecture and urbanism practice Gramazio & Kohler. Their award-winning works include the *Gantenbein* vineyard façade, the *Tanzhaus* theatre for contemporary dance, the Christmas lights for the *Bahnhofstrasse* in Zurich and the *sWISH** Pavilion at the Swiss National Exposition *Expo.02*.

Since 2005 Matthias Kohler and Fabio Gramazio have been assistant professors of *Architecture and Digital Fabrication* at the ETH Zurich Faculty of Architecture. Their research and teaching focus on architectural design strategies for full-scale robotic fabrication. Highly informed architectural elements are explored for their sensual, constructive and economic potential. They initiated the first robotic research lab in 2005 and the first transportable robotic unit for on-site fabrication in 2008.

MARC ANGÉLIL (1954) is an architect, teacher and scholar. He holds a Master of Architecture and a Doctor of Technical Sciences from the ETH Zurich, where he is currently a tenured professor in the Department of Architecture.

BERNARD CACHE (1958) is an architect and philosopher, and holds degrees from the Swiss Federal Polytechnic in Lausanne (1983) and the Polytechnical Institute of Philosophy at the University of Paris VIII.

OLIVER DOMEISEN (1969) AA dipl. produces, teaches, curates and writes about architecture. Director of dlm architectural designers ltd since 2000. Unit master Diploma/Intermediate School and VSP Architectural Assoc. London since 2001 Most recently curator of the Re-Sampling Ornament exhibition at the Swiss Architecture Museum.

BRENDA LYNN EDGAR (1972) studied architecture at the Rhode Island School of Design (1996), and Urban Design at Harvard University (1998). She holds a Master's in Architectural History from the University of Paris I, Panthéon-Sorbonne where she is currently pursuing a PhD.

TIM EDLER (1965) is a practicing architect and digital media specialist. He obtained his architectural diploma in 1994 from the Technical University of Berlin. Professor for "digital media studies" at the University of the Arts Bremen from 2005–2008.

MICHAEL FOX (1967) is an architect and founding partner of Los Angeles based firm Foxlin Inc. In 1998, Fox founded the Kinetic Design Group at the Massachusetts Institute of Technology (MIT), which he directed for three years. He currently lives in Los Angeles and is an assistant Professor of Architecture at Cal Poly Pomona.

GEORG FRANCK (1946) studied philosophy, economics and architecture. He holds a PhD in economics, and has practised as an architect and town-planner. Since 1994 he has held the chair of digital methods in architecture and planning at the Vienna University of Technology.

JOHN HAMILTON FRAZER (1945) is Professor and Head of School of Design at Queensland University of Technology. He is a Fellow of the Royal Society of Arts and a Fellow of the Chartered Society of Designers. He founded Autotectonica and was Chairman of the award winning Autographics software development company.

MANFRED GROHMANN (1953) is a civil engineer who holds degrees from Darmstadt Technical University. He has been Professor for Structural Design at Kassel University since 1996. He currently practices with Bollinger + Grohmann Engineers in Frankfurt am Main, which he co-founded in 1983.

MICHAEL HANAK (1968), a freelance art and architecture historian, journalist, curator and lecturer. He holds a degree in the history of art, film sciences and journalism from the University of Zurich. He is currently responsible for Public Relations at Gramazio & Kohler's chair of Architecture and Digital Fabrication.

SEAN KELLER (1970) is an architectural historian. He studied architecture at Princeton University, and at Harvard University, where he completed his PhD in 2005. He has taught architectural design, history and theory at Harvard and Yale Universities, and is currently an Assistant Professor in the College of Architecture at the Illinois Institute of Technology in Chicago.

AXEL KILIAN is an architect and scholar, and runs the design consultancy designexplorer. He holds a degree from the University of the Arts in Berlin, Germany and a Master of Science in Architectural Studies and a PhD in Computation from the Massachusetts Institute of Technology (MIT) and is now Assistant Professor at Delft University of Technology.

BRANKO KOLAREVIC (1963) is a designer and scholar working in the field of digital design and fabrication. He is a past president of ACADIA (Association for Computer Aided Design in Architecture) and holds a degree in architecture from the University of Belgrade as well as a Masters and Doctor of Design from Harvard University Graduate School of Design. He currently holds the Haworth Chair in Integrated Design at the University of Calgary.

NEIL LEACH is an architect and theorist. He is Professor of Architectural Theory at the University of Brighton, and has also taught at the Architectural Association, Columbia GSAPP Cornell University, Dessau Institute of Architecture and SCI-Arc.

CHRIS LUEBKEMAN (1961) is a civil engineer. He is currently the Director for Global Foresight and Innovation at Arup, London. He holds a degree in engineering from Vanderbilt University, a Masters of Science from Cornell University and a Doctor of Technical Sciences from the ETH Zurich.

ACHIM MENGES (1975) studied at the Architectural Association in London. He is Professor at Stuttgart University holding the chair for Computational Design and Studio Master of the Emergent Technologies and Design MSc/MArch Program at the AA in London. His work has been widely published and exhibited in Europe, North America and Asia. He is vice chairman of the international design research network OCEAN.

ÁKOS MORAVÁNSZKY (1950) is an architect and historian. He studied architecture at the Technical University in Budapest. In 1980, he completed a PhD in art history and historic preservation at the Technical University in Vienna. He was a research fellow at the Zentralinstitut für Kunstgeschichte in Munich, at the Getty Center in Santa Monica and taught as a Visiting Professor at the MIT (Cambridge, Mass.) and at the University of Applied Art in Budapest.

PHILIPPE MOREL (1973) is an architect and founding partner of Paris based firm EZCT Architecture & Design Research. He is also an Associate Professor at the Ecole Nationale Supérieure d'Architecture, Paris-Malaquais.

LARS MÜLLER (1955) designer and publisher, lives and works in Switzerland. Since 1982 he has been running a studio for visual communication. Since 1985 he has taught regularly. Founded Lars Müller Publishers in 1983, active in publishing in the fields of architecture, design, art, photography, and society, with an international focus.

PHILIPPE RAHM (1967) is an architect currently working in Paris and Lausanne. He studied at the Swiss Federal Institute of Technology (ETH) in Lausanne and Zurich and obtained his architectural diploma in 1993.

FRANÇOIS ROCHE (1961) is the founding partner of the Parisian architecture office R&Sie(n) with Stéphanie Lavaux. He obtained a diploma in 1987 form the French National School of Architecture at Versailles. He is currently teaching at Columbia University.

JULES SPINATSCH (1964) is an artist. His work has been exhibited at the New York MOMA, Haus der Kunst in Munich, Rotterdam's NAI, and at the Tate Modern in London. He lives in Zurich and teaches at Haute Ecole Art et Design HEAD, in Geneva.

LAURENT STALDER (1970) is currently assistant professor for the theory of architecture at the Swiss Federal Institute of Technology in Zurich (ETH). After obtaining his PhD in history of architecture at the ETH in 2002, he was until 2005 assistant professor at Laval University/Canada.

OLIVER TESSMANN (1973) studied architecture at the University of Kassel's School where he obtained his diploma in 2001. He has worked as an architect and a research assistant in structural design at the Kassel University and is currently working for Bollinger + Grohmann Engineers in Frankfurt am Main.

GEORGES TEYSSOT (1946) is an architect and scholar and has taught history and theory at the Istituto Universitario di Architettura of Venice (I.U.A.V.) in Italy, and at Princeton University's School of Architecture. He is currently Professor at Laval University's School of Architecture in Quebec, Canada.

PHILIP URSPRUNG (1963) is Professor of modern and contemporary art at the University of Zurich. From 1983–1993 he studied art history, general history and German in Geneva, Vienna and Berlin, gaining his doctorate in 1993, and his habilitation in 1999.

First, we would like to thank Lars Müller for inviting us to produce this book. It was an enriching experience for us to go through the process of what he calls "cooking a book" out of the various "ingredients," which we selected from the early years of our practice. Second, we offer our sincere thanks to the authors who contributed their thoughtful interjections in the form of probing questions, a cut through the visual history of robotics, and an essay on the same subject. We would like to emphasize that this book and the projects it presents were made possible through the immense commitment and innovative spirit of our collaborators, students and project partners. In addition to all those who contributed their professional skills, we also want to send a warm "thank you" to our friends and families for their love and support. Financially this book was made possible through the generous support of the ETH Zurich Faculty of Architecture, Keller Ziegeleien, KUKA Robot Switzerland, the Holcim Foundation and Pro Helvetia.

Fabio Gramazio, Matthias Kohler

DARCH ETH
Eidgenössische Technische Hochschule Zürich
Swiss Federal Institute of Technology Zurich

Keller
Building with system

KUKA

Holcim foundation
for sustainable construction

prohelvetia

DIGITAL MATERIALITY IN ARCHITECTURE
GRAMAZIO & KOHLER

Design: Integral Lars Müller/Séverine Mailler, Lars Müller
Project management: Michael Hanak
Project descriptions: Tobias Bonwetsch
Interjections editing: Brenda Lynn Edgar
Copy editing: Kirsten Weiss, Christa Zeller
Translations: Laura Bruce, Monica Buckland
Proofreading: Raymond Peat
Image editing: Michael Lyrenmann, Chantal Reichenbach
Production: Marion Plassmann
Printing and binding: Kösel, GmbH & Co. KG, Altusried-Krugzell
Litho: Sturm AG, Muttenz

Thanks to Trix Barmettler, Reto Geiser, Karin Grob, Kerstin Höger, Rasmus Joergensen, Roman Keller, Esther Kohler, Tobias Lutz, Marc Schwarz, Jürgen Strauss, Christian Waldvogel, Miriam Zehnder, Viola Zimmermann.

Photos: Alessandra Bello, Venice: pp. 103, 106, 108, 109.
Ralph Feiner, Malans: pp. 96/97, 98 below, 99 above, 100/101.
Roman Keller, Zurich: pp. 20 below, 21, 26 below, 27 below, 29, 30 bottom, 34, 36–41, 44 above, 45–47.
Michael Lyrenmann, Gramazio & Kohler, ETH Zurich: pp. 48–87, 98 middle, 104/105, 107.
All others by Gramazio & Kohler, Zurich

Plans and diagrams: Gregor Bieri, Stefan Bischof, p. 64
Daniel Hässig, Aline Vuilliomenet, p. 66 above
Yuta Kanezuka, Sibèlle Urben, p. 66 middle
Christoph Rauhut, p. 66 below
Christian Blasimann, Barbara Zwicky, p. 68 above left
Kathrin Hasler, Christoph Junk, Hannes Oswald, p. 68 above right
Michael Bühler, David Dalsass, Simon Filler, Roman Kallweit, Jonathan Roider, p. 72
Ladina Esslinger, Chris Keller, p. 80
All others by Gramazio & Kohler, Zurich

Robocrop foldout: Jules Spinatsch, Zurich: pp. 51–54 (Copyright 2007 © by Jules Spinatsch; Copyright by Corbis: p. 54 right; Getty Images: p. 53 right bottom; Keystone Switzerland: p. 51 right. Special thanks are due to Keystone and to all photographers whose pictures have been used here, as well as to the inventors of photography and the Internet.

Lars Müller Publishers
Baden, Switzerland
www.lars-muller-publishers.com

ISBN 978-3-03778-122-7

Printed in Germany

© 2008 Lars Müller Publishers
No part of this book may be used or reproduced in any form or manner whatsoever without prior written permission except in the case of brief quotations embodied in critical articles and reviews.